NO MOON TONIGHT

Don Charlwood

A Goodall paperback
from
Crécy Publishing Limited

First published in paperback by Goodall in 1984
Reprinted 1995
This edition published in 2000

ISBN 0 907579 97 3

946.5441
1447233

Printed by Interprint, Malta

A Goodall paperback

published by

Crécy Publishing Limited
1a Ringway Trading Estate, Shadowmoss Road, Manchester M22 5LH

Contents

Acknowledgements

The publishers thank Mrs H. M. Davies and Jonathan Cape Limited for permission to print an extract used by the author from *The Collected Poems of W. H. Davies*.

Foreword

BY AIR VICE-MARSHAL D. C. T. BENNETT CB, CBE, DSO

No Moon Tonight is a book of deep feelings. It depicts with stark simplicity the fears and hopes, the courage and the tenacity of the aircrews of Bomber Command. It tells of their great and vitally important sacrifice. They struck directly at the enemy, with strength far exceeding anything previously known.

May the true British, of Don Charlwood's Australia, of Canada, New Zealand, South Africa, Rhodesia and the Old · Country itself, remember and cherish their bravery and continue to fight for the freedom – nationally and personally – for which we all fought.

Don Bennett
Leader of the Pathfinders

Preface

In 1944, during enforced leisure in a Canadian military hospital, I began to make detailed notes from diaries and letters and from my memories of our previous winter with Bomber Command. The notes were the basis of this book, but I was long in the writing of it. Like most of those who returned from the war, I married, found a job — with civil air traffic control — and had a family. Also, I laboured on the building of our own home. *No Moon Tonight* did not appear until 1956. It was my first book.

Like Coleridge's Ancient Mariner, I had had the compulsion to tell a tale of an unforgettable experience, small though my part in it had been. During the winter of 1942-43, on 103 Squadron, Elsham Wolds, it had struck me that the public heard much about the outstanding men of Bomber Command — those I have referred to as the 'Himalayan men' — but little about ordinary aircrew; much about the Command's successes, little about the cost in lives. During the war it was understandable that this was so, but the tendency continued after the war was over. I felt a need to paint the other side of our life — our inner life. I realized that to do this honestly, I would have to tell of things as they had seemed to me, for in those days one was only occasionally privy to the inner thoughts and feelings of others.

When the book was written and the proofs came to me for checking, I felt embarrassed as I read in chill print the exposure of so much that I had previously concealed. I was tempted to make large cuts, but the time for that was past; I had to leave the pages as they were. In the end I was glad I had done so, not only because the book was kindly received both in the United Kingdom and here in Australia, but because numerous letters from ex-aircrew men began to tell me I had not been alone in my response to the Bomber Command experience.

Our generation never really emerged from the shadow of the First World War, that cataclysmic 'war to end war.' The rise of Nazism was a lengthening of the same shadow over our youth. When this threat was faced by Britain in 1939, the response in Australia was not only that we, too, must face Nazism, but that we must stand by the threatened 'Homeland.' I expect that this was so in other Commonwealth countries too. I use the term 'Homeland' now in inverted commas because, in Australia today, it is an anachronism. In 1939 we were a country of predominantly British stock; today Australia is a multi-racial nation, its bonds with Britain diminished. Britain, likewise, has turned from her Dominions to forge bonds with the countries of the European continent. Nevertheless, it is not surprising that our generation sometimes feels nostalgic for the close-knit family of nations we remember.

My own feelings for Britain and her people are evident enough in these pages. They were shared, I believe, by most wartime air force men whose homes lay outside the British Isles. We found ourselves caught up in the remarkable feeling of unity that pervaded the land in those years. Ever since then we have laid claim to a subtler level of British citizenship than can be conferred by passport.

Most of us came to Britain through the Empire Air Training Scheme, an imaginative and remarkably successful scheme now too little remembered. I was one of the many Australians trained in Canada; indeed, in 1944 I married there. My Australian pilot on 103 Squadron trained at home under the same scheme; many of my Initial Training Course trained in the Rhodesia of those years.

I have always been glad that 103 was a 'mixed' squadron and our own a 'mixed' crew, though not a crew of such diverse origins as many were. Nothing proved a better corrective to excessive national pride than to find that each country produced its own quota of courageous and capable men, loyal to those with whom they flew. And I fancy that a mixed crew might have been predisposed to good performance. One was inclined to think, 'If this Englishman — or Canadian, or Dutchman, or New Zealander — can cope with this job, then so can I.'

There has been an RAF Elsham Wolds Association in existence since 1979. It holds biennial reunions of men and women who served in wartime either with 103 Squadron, or with its offspring of November 1943, 576 Squadron. These gatherings open at the aerodrome site with a service and a fly-past. Although much of the aerodrome has now reverted to farmland and part of it is an industrial estate, a memorial and a Garden of Remembrance have been established to the station's thousand dead. It is there that the opening ceremony is held — a most moving occasion, as all the surviving members of our crew can testify.

My Australian publisher discontinued distribution of *No Moon Tonight* in Britain several years ago. I am heartened now by the appearance of this new edition and am happy to be in the company of Goodall's air force authors. When I wrote the book I felt obliged to conceal the identity of several men by use of pseudonyms. In this edition I have been afforded opportunity to give their actual names. I remember the characters of these pages as if the drama had been yesterday; remember them as eternally young. All honour to them!

DON CHARLWOOD
TEMPLESTOWE, VICTORIA, 1984

CHAPTER ONE

Retrospect

The train left Aberdeen in the late afternoon and by the time we reached Stonehaven it was dusk. As I watched the North Sea beating at the Scottish cliffs and heard the shriek of the wind about the train, I realized that I might never again see this bleak expanse of water; certainly never from the air, perhaps never from the shore. Often we had looked down on it as darkness fell and we sped eastward to a waiting Germany; we had only felt affection for it when I was able to say to the crew, 'We have crossed the enemy coast and are well out to sea.' I used to feel then that everyone had sighed deeply. Down would go our nose and within forty minutes we would see the searchlights of England.

This same sea they said had claimed Tom and Max and God only knew how many others from among my friends. Now, I alone of all of them was going home.

A porter drew the blackout curtain, leaving only the wind to remind me of the scene outside ....

Sometimes in later years that last glimpse of the North Sea returned to me, but the emotions it represented, I almost forgot. I even forgot how we had felt as we had watched for the Ruhr, crouched ahead of us in the darkness. Then one day long after, without knowing why, I became afraid. The other life began crowding back, until suddenly I realized that I was listening to a song we had known ten years before. Even as I listened my surroundings dissolved and the song became a worn recording, an arrangement of "Tristesse" played on a gramophone.

I knew then that we were in the mess at Elsham Wolds on a night in January 1943. About me were many men I had known, most of them now ten years dead. There were Laing and Webber; Newitt and Berry; Maddern, our own pilot, and with him Richards, our Welsh engineer. They wore heavy white sweaters under their battle dress and each carried on his collar a silver whistle. Tonight we were to go to Düsseldorf. They were sending only thirty bombers from the whole Command, for it was to be an experiment that might easily fail.

On the faces of the men about me there was a similarity of expression, an expression I had often called 'contemptuous serenity.' They spoke very little and when they did their voices were subdued, as though at the same time they were listening.

I wondered why it was that this recording happened to be played so often as we waited to leave. To me it was a song without hope, full of urgent pleadings we could never heed.

I sat at a corner table finishing a letter home, as I had often done while we waited to leave. Familiar sounds registered on my mind as they had done before: the clack of billiard balls, rain on the windows and the unrelenting song.

Soon the crews about me began leaving. In their hands they carried red packages of escape equipment — tabloid foods, maps printed on silk, a small compass — in case tonight they were shot down, but survived. It occurred to me how young they were and how foreign to their task. There was Morris, who at nineteen was so soon to die, and Syd Cook, now a sergeant, but in the year of life left him to rise to Squadron Leader and be doubly decorated. And Ian Robb, the first among those I knew who was not to return. Other men lay dozing in the long green chairs. As members of their crews roused them I noticed how child-like they appeared in the moment they woke. I saw them leaving the mess. Outside the rain had increased and as they passed through the door they put on their coats and turned up their collars.

With a feeling of urgency I turned back to my letter.

'It is time now to go. Geoff and the rest of the crew have already left and except for a few ground staff men I am alone in the mess. Once again it scarcely seems possible that we will leave this room, with its chairs and fire, for the grey miles of the North Sea, then Germany.'

I paused, not knowing how to end. The imploring crescendo of the song filled the room. In a moment of defiance I wrote quickly, 'Whatever happens, I feel that when all is known, all will be well.'

Between the inner and outer doors I paused. Outside the night was empty and very dark, the rain heavier. I shuddered and pulled on my coat. As I left the building the last words of the song followed me, as on other nights they had followed other men now no longer there,

'No moon tonight,
No moon tonight.'

CHAPTER TWO

This England

As we pulled over a bare hill I saw ahead of us a shepherd driving sheep. For a moment he stared at the Anson with terror, then flung himself on his face, while his flock scattered among the rocks. At this the pilot laughed uproariously. Recalling the purpose of our exercise he shouted, 'Very well, navigator, where are we now?'

I pointed unsteadily to a village. 'Corwen,' I said.

'Correct!' He swung away from it, drawing the flesh from my face. 'Wales is my native land,' he announced grandly. 'On map-reading exercises I come here invariably.'

He was a black-haired Flying Officer with moustaches that stood out like brushes on either side of his face. Over his pocket he wore the faded ribbon of a DFM. His life, we had heard, was a constant battle to escape from Training Command and return to operations.

'What is in the valley to port?'

'A lake.'

'Its name?'

'Bala.'

'Yes, yes; Bala. Also called Llyn Tegid. You have done well,' he mused — 'very well.' His moustaches expressed his approval. 'I think now we shall go back.'

He climbed to 1,000ft, but on the way home his fancy was taken by a small town.

'What place is this?'

At first I failed to identify it.

'Quickly!'

He had dropped one wing and was pointing along it to buildings which were growing in size each second. I saw white, upturned faces in the single street and a bicycle leaning against a post.

With an effort I said, 'Dolgelly'.

'"Dol-gelly",' he mimicked. 'Yeh, yeh. Correct.'

He asked no more, but turned south-west for Hereford and the Severn Valley. On the last miles to the river we pulled up to cross a succession of hedges and banked frequently to pass between trees. Ahead then lay the water, shaded from the afternoon sun. We followed its every turning, our slipstream fanning its surface. Feeling more secure I gazed into the green hearts of willows and on to sinuous paths beside the water. As we turned for the Wrekin, which was our guide to Bobbington, I thought, 'To be afraid was foolish. If this pilot doesn't value my life, at least he values his own.' But a week later he gleefully killed himself on a low-level cross-country flight in Wales.

We had come to Bobbington to familiarize ourselves with English flying conditions and this was our last flight. We were quartered in tents on a slope at the bottom of the camp. In the evening lull that night, when day flying was over and before night flying had begun, I lay with the sides of our tent rolled, listening to the bleating of ewes and lambs in the adjoining fields.

Keith Webber of the Twenty Men lifted the flap of the tent. He was older than most of us, tall and a little stooped.

'Feel like a walk?'

'Yes,' I said.

We climbed through the boundary fence and walked towards a small wood at the top of a nearby hill. In many ways Keith typified navigators. As a group they tended more to seriousness than the men they flew with. There were, of course, exceptions. Among the Twenty we had 'Blue' Freeman, whose activities were once mentioned in the House of Commons. This was after he had set fire to a Land Army cottage on display in Trafalgar Square.

'Blue' had turned nineteen during our training in Canada; Keith was now thirty. The Twenty had left Australia together in 1941 and had trained in Canada. Eighteen were destined for Bomber Command. At the end, five of these had come through, one was a prisoner of war and twelve were dead.

That is to say, they were an average group; perhaps a little better than average.

With Keith Webber I walked up the slope to the small wood at its head.

'I suppose,' said Keith, 'it would be called a "coppice", or "copse".'

He repeated these unfamiliar words slowly, as though savouring them. From somewhere ahead we heard a cuckoo. We stood in the long grass waiting for the call to be repeated, but the bird remained silent, leaving only a hum of insects in the still air.

Next day we were to leave for an Operational Training Unit. There the Twenty Men would split, each man going to a crew. After that came a Squadron. When I thought of this and wondered how I would meet the impact of operational life, I felt a spasm of fear. I glanced at Keith, but he was absorbed in his discoveries, his mind far from the things I had remembered.

We had come into the wood by a crooked path. The air there was cool and the light as green as the sea. Presently the cuckoo began calling again, but always it sounded far away, not only in body, but strangely far in spirit, as though it told of English springs long passed.

CHAPTER THREE

OTU Lichfield

W e had been posted to No. 27 Operational Training Unit, Lichfield. The atmosphere there was different from anything we had known, for at Lichfield all instructors had completed a tour. Furthermore, at the end of our training as crews we went on a flap.

'What is a flap?'

'A flap? Oh, a full moon do. The first was the thousand bomber raid on Cologne. Every kite that can fly is sent. They're called flaps because everyone from the Wingco down flaps about 'em for weeks. There's one tonight.'

'Tonight?' We had talked ops for a year, but always they had belonged to another place, another time. And now — 'Tonight.'

In the sergeants' mess that evening we saw the men who were to go. They had already put on their flying kit — white sweaters under their battle dress and fleece-lined boots that scraped heavily on the floor. I had known many of them in Canada, but tonight they were in a world so far removed from ours that they appeared strangers. In the morning they would have solved the riddles that beset us: What were ops really like? What did it feel like to see flak? to look down on the enemy coast? to see the target? Watching them, these things seemed far away. Outside lay fields and distant spires; cuckoos called and a horse grazed slowly within our sight.

As dusk came the men began leaving. We knew neither their target nor their time of take-off. For an hour we were left sitting in the mess, waiting and listening. The horse still grazed in the half light; the sky beyond the spires was darkening.

Then, as though at a signal, all Lichfield began quivering with sound. A dozen pilots were running up their engines, checking them thoroughly. The horse lifted its head, then turned again to the grass. The men sitting in the mess glanced from their books and their beer into the failing light.

On a sudden impulse I got up and went down to the aerodrome. The whole evening vibrated urgently there with the drumming of motors. Lights were twinkling over the wide expanse of grass, guiding the aircraft to their positions. Dimly I could see a line of Wellingtons waiting at the northern end of the 'drome. I tried to visualize again the men I had seen in the mess and to imagine their thoughts as they waited. But all this was new to me and I experienced nothing more than tension and foreboding. The leading aircraft left the head of the line and stood facing into wind, pausing there as though scenting the air. Its roaring suddenly intensified; it moved forward; gathered speed. Its effort to leave the ground at first appeared unavailing, but near the end of the runway it lifted heavily. As it skimmed the trees, a second Wellington followed it, then a third. I stood against a hangar wall watching them closely, clenching my hands as though plunging with them into the unknown. Each aircraft followed in quick succession, till all had gone, leaving a throb of motors on the still air. The only light now was in the dome of the sky where the 'planes were circling, climbing steadily to operating altitude. There was a hollow sound to their roaring as they became smaller and smaller above the earth.

I was walking slowly back to the mess, when I heard two instructors as they passed on their bicycles.

'Can't say I'm sorry not to be on tonight. These Wimps have had their time.'

'Yes, I don't even like them on cross countries.'

It was soon completely dark, the sky swept with the first pale stars.

That night German bombers attacked Birmingham and Derby. I woke up, listening. The bombs sounded far away, but occasionally a bomber passed overhead, its desynchronized engines droning through the night. Above our beds an amplified voice cried, 'The air raid warning is red! The air raid warning is red!' But no one in the hut moved or spoke.

When we rose, the men who had gone on the flap were sleeping, but news of them had already reached us. One crew was missing. We remembered them vaguely from the night before, chiefly because one of their number had grumbled at the lack of Australian mail. There was mail for him now, but by lunch time it had been taken from the rack. That was all there was to it. Scarcely a ripple was caused on the surface of the station's life. The men who had been on the flap rose for lunch. They stood talking in small groups, enveloped by the gaiety of released tension. They were talking freely, but our questions they were unable to answer. How did it feel? What was the navigation like? What was the flak like? Perhaps we had hoped that they would return with some message for us, but what the message could be, we did not ask ourselves. Had we done so, we might have realized that we wanted to know how we would feel; how we would manage the navigation; how we would react to flak, those haunting questions answerable only by ourselves in the time ahead.

Before lectures began the senior Lichfield officers introduced themselves. These men with their ribbons, their moustaches and their slang gripped our imagination. They had operated, they were skilled, they had about them an elusive air — something I could never define. Perhaps it sprang from their attitude to action. They were still geared to operational pitch and were endlessly scheming to get back to a squadron. Not to get back because they were patriots, or because they imagined themselves to be heroes, but because 'dicing' in the fellowship of a squadron had intoxicated them. By this they not only won us to the RAF but, unwittingly, imparted to us a little of their spirit.

That night we were allotted barracks near the mess. I roomed with Harry Wright, of the Twenty Men, the untidiest, most generous, least promising-looking man among us. He was a Queenslander and spoke with a pronounced Australian accent. The further we travelled from Australia, the stronger his accent became, as though in this way he exhibited loyalty to his homeland. With his black, unshorn hair, his worried eyes, his pale cadaverous face, he might have been anything between twenty and thirty. He was actually twenty-one, and in civil life a draughtsman. He unpacked his kitbag, whistling tunelessly. Everything that he failed to jam into the drawers of our dressing table he threw under his bed, until he had an assortment there of hampers from home; books; an Australian slouch hat; sketches he had done in his spare time; unopened laundry; dirty clothes; writing materials and, lastly, a boomerang. I looked at this enquiringly.

'T' bring me back. I'm goin' t' write my ops on it as I do 'em.'

He picked it up thoughtfully and fixed it on the wall over the head of his bed.

In the morning, as we prepared to leave for the lecture rooms, he selected from under his bed a copy of *War and Peace*, the writing materials and a packet of biscuits from a hamper. The book and the writing materials he stuffed down the front of his battle dress, the biscuits he munched for breakfast on his way to class.

Lectures were over, ended for all time. This was my life for evermore. We had taken off after dark and were headed for the core of a storm. The other aircraft had been recalled, but somehow the signal had not reached us. The Anson leapt upward, yawed and plunged like a ship at sea. Beside the pilot sat a bomb aimer, the first bomb aimer I had flown with. He had introduced himself as Ted Batten, a tall, blond Londoner, in civil life an optician. Now he sat with a topographical map spread on his knees, trying to obtain pinpoints for my use in navigation. After a time he came lurching back to me.

'I can't get a glimpse of the ground at all. If this stuff breaks I'll let you know.'

As he spoke the cloud about us was weirdly illumined,

then plunged again into darkness.

'We're going to be for it,' I said.

'Hm, rather murky.' He glanced downward, then back to his map with apparent unconcern, but shook his head regretfully.

'By the way, what's the height to be?'

'Six thousand feet,' I said.

'Good; Snowdon plus a couple of thousand — just as well, too.'

We were flying first to Rhyl and then to St Bees Head. He clambered to his seat beside the pilot, becoming one of two silhouettes against the lightning.

I tapped the W.Op. on the shoulder. 'Any hope of bearings?'

'Eh?'

'Are you able to get any bearings?'

'Just listen to the bloody static!'

He jammed a head-phone against my ear. I shrugged and returned to the chart. The cloud about us was illumined almost continually and writing was barely possible. Clinging to the desk, I knew that it would not be long before I was sick.

On our estimated time of arrival at Rhyl, the W.Op. unexpectedly produced a bearing on Aldergrove. It indicated that we were crossing the coast west of track. I told this to Ted and together we stared below. As we watched, a momentary break appeared. Through it, in the first light of the dawn, we saw a coastline running north-west and south-east, off our port bow.

'The west side of Colwyn Bay!' I said.

Ted didn't answer, but looked at his map, then out of the window again, considering the two as he might have considered an elderly client for spectacles.

I hurried back to alter course eastward. I was bringing the alteration to the pilot, written on a piece of paper, when Ted shouted, 'That isn't Colwyn Bay, it's the west side of the Dee!'

He was staring downward. 'You can see it now. We're drifting eastward from it pretty quickly.'

Pale below I saw the estuary of the Dee. We were drifting uncomfortably close to Liverpool, a city that considered all aircraft to be German. I gave the pilot a temporary alteration of course, then worked out the wind. It was almost due west at over 50 knots. The cloud closed again quickly, pounding us until it drove me to the rear window. I opened it and let the slipstream whip my face. We had come into clear air above shreds of the storm. Six thousand feet below, the sea heaved and broke in the half light. Behind us the mountains of Wales were indistinct through scud. That my gift to these seas was Welsh rabbit seemed appropriate, even at this most miserable hour.

Ted came back and stooped over me.

'We've lost an engine! What's the nearest 'drome?'

I muttered that I little cared.

'Shall I work out the course for you?' He was still polite and deliberate.

I shook my head and returned to the table. The nearest aerodrome was Silloth. I worked out a course; gave it to the pilot and scrambled back to the window.

Slowly the nausea was swept away by the cold air. It was succeeded by a wave of shame and the realization that our Anson might crash into the sea. We were losing height gradually, but as we crossed the coast and joined the Silloth circuit, our engine picked up and the pilot asked for a course home. As we landed half an hour later, both engines cut, nor were they started again for nearly a week.

Ted Batten and I walked together to the mess. Within twenty-four hours we were to be in the same crew, but as we left the Anson behind us that morning, we were oblivious to our future.

By afternoon the storm had passed. We were at the Lichfield satellite of Tatenhill, a place with an unvarying menu of Welsh rabbit. Rather than face this again for tea I resolved to cycle into the country. I took a road northward between fields of wheat and occasional woods and came at length to an inn called 'The Swan.' Nearby a farmer stood examining his crop to see if it was ready to cut. With him, my first Englishman encountered on his native soil, I fell into conversation. His name was Gordon Hardwick, his farm was called Toby's Hill Farm, and the name of the place where we stood was Draycott-in-the-Clay.

When we parted I began riding towards strangely shaped hills that rose abruptly from the surrounding country. The highest of these hills was wooded and above the trees rose the square tower of a church. I made for this hill by any lane that appeared to lead towards it, and in twenty minutes was climbing it slowly. It soon forced me to walk, but near the top the road turned and levelled and I rode into a hilltop village that from below had been screened by trees. I passed an inn with a fighting cock on its board and came to the church. In a cottage opposite a man and his wife sat at tea, the man tilting his chair back to glance at me through the open door. I stopped and asked him the name of the village.

'Hanbury,' he said, getting up. 'The church is very old — they say a thousand years.'

He came to his gate and we stood leaning there talking.

'They say the Queen of the Danes died here during one of their raids. When the Danes came back for her body, the people hurried overland with it to Chester. It's there now, they say — we never got it back.' While we stood there his wife joined us, bringing with her a glass of gooseberry wine and a piece of cake. She smiled as she handed them to me. She said, 'What we would do without you boys, I don't know.'

The words were spoken so simply that I, who had seen no action, could find no answer. Their vicar, they told me, had a son somewhere in Australia; no doubt he would be glad if he could meet me. As it was Sunday, I decided to wait for Evensong.

I waited under an oak in the churchyard, facing out towards the soft complexity of fields and hedges of the lower country. I had almost fallen asleep there when I heard the sound of feet on the churchyard path. The congregation was small and most of the people were old. They listened intently to the sonorous voice of their vicar, their minds perhaps wavering between his words and their memories of the young, who were no longer with them.

'And I said, Oh that I had wings like a dove!
Then would I fly away and be at rest.
Lo, then would I wander far off
And lodge in the wilderness.'

When the service had ended the vicar led me to a half-timbered vicarage on the edge of the hill. We went into a room I have always remembered. Its tall windows faced west, looking down to the fields and villages of the lower neighbourhood and across them to the Pennines. The low sun filled it with light and peace. The vicar's son was in Geraldton, Western Australia, so far from my home that I could do nothing to bring his distant parish clearly to his parents' eyes. We sat to a supper of cold lamb and tomatoes and peas from the vicarage garden.

In the morning I was confronted by a rather short, untidy sergeant pilot, whose bearing was an affront to the Air Force. His eyes and the depressed corners of his mouth were sardonic, almost grim. I knew him as Geoff Maddern. He removed a drooping, hand-rolled cigarette from his lips and addressed me sharply.

'Are you flying with anyone?'

'No,' I said.

'How about flying together?'

'OK,' I said.

At that we looked at each other closely, the same thought probably passing through the minds of us both, 'How will this man turn out in the business ahead?' Much later I was to hear Geoff called 'the personification of courage.' He was a West Australian, aged twenty-seven. Irascible and sardonic in appearance — and often in behaviour — Geoff was nevertheless to prove a happy companion. He rode a decrepit bicycle, painted grey. In character and appearance it was to remind me often of its rider. It knocked people down, ran into posts and, after parties, often left Geoff in the gutter. He called it 'The Grey Ghost.'

A few days after I had joined him, Geoff came to me leading a wispish Englishman with wide-open, brown eyes. On his head an ancient cap defied both gravity and Air Force regulations. His dark hair was slicked back and a cigarette hung from his mouth. He could be nothing other than a RAF gunner.

'This is Arthur Browett, our rear gunner. I'm calling him "Shag."'

The gunner nodded briefly, accepting the gratuitous nickname solemnly.

'What part are you from?' I asked, by way of conversation.

'Nottin'am.'

His brevity was disconcerting.

'Most of my time, though, I've been in the RAF,' he volunteered suddenly.

'In England?'

He nodded again. ''cept at the beginnin' — I was in France till they folded up.'

By this time Ted Batten had joined us as bomb aimer. We all went to the mess and there gradually loosened 'Shag's' tongue. After that we were never able to curb it.

The crew of a Wellington was five. We had a pilot, a navigator, a rear gunner and a bomb aimer. We were still without a wireless operator. I met a W/Op one day who had been held back through illness. His name was Max Burcher, an impetuous youngster from New South Wales. He had the restlessness of a caged tiger, as if in training he was behind bars and only in action could see promise of contentment. I asked him to join us, and in his eagerness he did so without question. Next day we flew together for the first time. We were not a crew, we were a 'plane load of bewildered individuals. We scraped over the balloon barrages of Rugby, Birmingham and Coventry and struggled home. A few days later we flew our first cross-country exercise. The intercom was a new toy that no one had advised us to use sparingly. Everything we said we repeated; we thought it made for clarity and it sounded dramatic. To concentrate on navigation during these exchanges was impossible. Besides this, I was stricken blind. In Ansons I had been able to check our position from ample windows. In my compartment in Wellingtons I could see nothing and was dependent on the bomb aimer for map-reading. An hour out we found ourselves above unbroken cloud. I opened the forward door and glanced over the billowing miles, wondering when we would catch a glimpse of the ground. Geoff sat solidly at the controls, more than usually sardonic-looking, his eyes puckered against the glare. We did not see the ground again for four hours. By this time we were due back over Lichfield and Geoff was fast losing patience.

'Navigator from pilot; navigator from pilot: when can I start descending? When can I start descending? Where the hell are we, anyway?'

'I'm just getting a check. Max is taking some bearings.'

'Don't you *know* where we are?'

'How can I? The radio has been U/S and we've been over cloud for four and a half hours!'

'Well, what do you want me to do? Stay on this damn' course? Our ETA is up.'

'Yes, stay on this course.'

I tapped Max. 'Any luck yet?'

'What?'

'Any luck?'

'Give a man a chance! I can hardly hear for static. Do you really need these bearings?'

'I haven't had a check——'

'You mean you're lost.'

'All right then, I'm lost; just get me some bearings!'

'You navigators seem to think W/Ops are your slaves.'
'Navigator from pilot; navigator from pilot. Listen, these bloody things don't fly on fresh air! We've got to get down. Get me a QDM or any damn' thing. I can't see the point in stooging on in this direction!'

I remembered 'Taffy' Davis, our Welsh navigation instructor: 'Now, dawn't let the crew get you rattled. If they all start shouting at you, just pool out your intercom plug and keep working quietly.' I pulled it out, enveloping myself in silence. Max presently handed me a piece of paper on which was scrawled, 'QBY Lichfield 202°', which was to say that we must steer 202° to reach Lichfield, but that balloons lay along our track. The problem was quickly solved. By five-thirty we were approaching Lichfield to land.

On the ground a transformation occurred. We became calm and tolerant. With a certain amount of shame we realized that we would have to develop these qualities in the air.

The desired state of calm and confidence came to us slowly. By the time our day flying was over we were still no more than 'stuff crews are made of.' We faced night exercises with misgivings. Five aircraft had been lost on night cross-country flights in a week. One had crashed into the streets of Fishguard; another had vanished into the North Sea; the rear gunner of a third had thought conditions 'extremely bumpy' until he had realized that the bumps were being caused by a hilltop; the fourth and fifth were mysteries. Five aircraft were a heavier loss, we were reminded, than the five crews.

During this week of accidents another of the Twenty Men arrived at Lichfield. Max Bryant was one of the youngest of the group and one of the most able. I had been his flying partner during our training in Canada and had sat beside him in class. He had come to the Air Force as a law student of twenty and had flung himself into training with enthusiasm that appalled me. While I laboured beside him to learn essentials, he absorbed details effortlessly. He was proud and ambitious but his pride and ambition were wrapped up in his supreme desire for efficiency in the air. As a result he arrived at Lichfield an officer, while I was still a sergeant. Not being known there, he rectified this in his own way. He took off his tunic and borrowed one of mine, then came with me to the sergeants' mess.

'What stage of your training are you up to?'

'Night cross-countries,' I said. 'We do the first tonight.'

He grasped my arm, 'Would you mind if I came?'

I laughed. 'Of course not!'

We were driven to the aircraft while it was still light. About the edge of the dispersal point, wheat had been cut and stooked so that the sheaves almost completely encircled the 'plane. I saw Max looking at the fields and the distant woods much as I had looked at England in my first unbelievable days there. As the aircraft was not ready, we settled with our backs against a stook. He said to me then: 'It seems impossible, doesn't it? — the war, I mean. I suppose the ops boys are waiting too.'

I said, 'I wonder what it's like to be whirled from a place like this to Germany?'

He considered for a time, then asked seriously, 'How many of us do you think will see next year out?'

I knew that he would have asked this of no one else. Perhaps because I was six years his senior, he questioned me as if I were a parent and he a child. Nearly always his questions left me with a feeling of inadequacy.

I could only reply, 'It's hard to guess.'

'What are the losses on each raid?'

'They say five per cent.'

'Five per cent and we do thirty ops.' He considered this thoughtfully. 'We sort of end up owing something.'

'You know,' he said then, 'one of the first things an instructor mentioned to us today was that we should go into ops with some definite belief to strengthen ourselves. For his part, he regarded this as a holy war.'

I wanted to make some cynical remark, but to Max I

could not. Besides, the fundamental idea of the instructor was right.

It was swiftly getting dark. Already bats were swooping between us and the first stars. Geoff and the others of the crew were hovering impatiently about the 'plane. Max nodded towards them.

'I wonder how they feel about things? I suppose you'll never know in all the time you're flying with them.'

'Never really, I suppose. I make guesses sometimes. Max Burcher is longing for action. When it comes I don't think anything will shake him. The whole show is a wizard adventure perhaps that's the best way to think of it too. Ted Batten and "Shag" are harder to fathom. "Shag" has his wife to think of and Ted is to be married before we go to a squadron. But they've never whispered a word of worry; I don't imagine they ever will.'

'What about Geoff?'

'I think he guesses what we're up against, but he keeps his knowledge in a bolted room at the back of his mind. Sometimes he looks at it, just to remind himself of his responsibilities, but he never lets it show in his face. He realizes how he must live to win our confidence and make a crew of us.'

'Some of the chaps make a man feel inadequate, don't they? As far as I'm concerned, sometimes I feel I'll be able to carry out anything; other times I'm morbid and scared.'

Q Queenie was ready. We left the wheat and climbed to our places.

Our night flights progressed so smoothly that it looked as if we would get away before the first full moon. On our leave we intended going as a crew to Ted's wedding in London. After, I planned to continue to Inverness and walk then to Fort William.

Lichfield — Rhyl — Douglas — Codling Bank — Great Ormes Head — Ternhill — Lichfield. With this flight our training ended. Next morning we were posted to the Halifaxes of 103 Squadron, Elsham Wolds, Lincolnshire.

Of the Twenty Men, Harry Wright, Keith Webber and 'Blue' Freeman were posted to the same squadron. That afternoon Ted Batten left for London to prepare for his wedding. I spent a subdued last evening at 'The Goat's Head' with Max Bryant. As we climbed the long hill back to the camp I felt as if time had undergone a subtle change. The week in Scotland stretched before me like half a lifetime.

We came in the main gate of the camp and pulled up on the road. By now it was dark, but in the moonlight I saw Johnnie Dodgshun, an Australian who lived near my parents' home in Melbourne, running toward the flight office.

'What's the panic?'

He looked back over his shoulder. 'There's a flap on tomorrow night.'

I felt a tingling along my spine. 'Who's going?'

'Twelve crews — yours is one of them.'

I ran to the barracks. The men there had evidently heard nothing of the flap, as most of them were packing for their leave. I took Geoff aside.

'We're on a flap tomorrow night.'

'What's that?'

Others about us glanced up, but returned unsuspectingly to their packing.

'Who told you?'

'Johnnie Dodgshun — he has it from the CGI.'

Geoff appeared about to explode with anger, but then I saw him accept the situation and make his first decision.

'I'll go and book a good kite. R Robert is about the best of a poor lot.'

He hurried out without his cap and rattled off on the 'Grey Ghost.'

Harry Wright looked at me enquiringly.

'There's a flap on tomorrow night,' I said. 'The whole course is on it.'

The mood about us changed swiftly to something elating but strangely unpleasant, as though suddenly we had been stripped to spiritual nakedness. Half laughingly men began to write 'last letters.' Caught by their mood, I took a pad and went to Max Bryant's room. I found Max preparing for bed.

'It's on, then?'

I nodded and explained what I wanted.

'I'll turn in, but you go right ahead. Help yourself to whatever you want.'

I drew a chair to his table and adjusted his reading lamp. He wandered out with a towel over his shoulder and his toothbrush between his teeth. I knew Max's daily ritual almost as well as I knew my own. Seeing him as I saw him now was to be taken back to the days of a few months before, when he had slept in a top bunk and I below and outside our window had lain quiet Canadian snow. When he returned I said to him, 'I'll leave this on your table. Could you post it if needs be?'

'Of course — but nothing will go wrong. Somehow I have a hunch you'll come through your tour.'

'Thirty ops? It's a forbidding sort of total.'

'And yet, it's not a cumulative risk. Actually a man runs no more risk on his tenth than he does on his first. In fact, the further he goes the better his chances should become.'

I could see that this was a theory he had argued often with himself, but it was far from convincing. He looked at me in that challenging way of his. I laughed shortly.

'All right. We'll all get through.'

'We might, too. Somehow I think we're going to be a lucky flight.'

Max had been asleep for over an hour when I finished the letter and left it on his table. His face was relaxed, glowing still from his shower.

Our barracks were in darkness, but the blackout curtain between Harry's bed and mine was drawn aside, admitting the light of a full moon. I went to bed enumerating the things that must be done next day. My flying clothing would have to be unpacked; the navigator's compartment of R Robert would have to be checked; I must see that the astro-dome could be jettisoned easily in case tomorrow night we had to ditch.

'In case we have to ditch.'

The thought caused me to hold my breath. I looked suddenly at Harry, feeling that he might have observed my spasm of fear, but he was sleeping soundly, breathing easily, as though tomorrow we were still to go on leave.

I began to realize that this moment was something I had never really believed. Though we had trained for Germany and talked of Germany and had seen men go out and fail to return, our own departure was something before which my imagination had always halted. Now the RAF had said, 'We are teaching you no more. Armed with your present knowledge, you are to navigate a 'plane to Germany. If your knowledge is inadequate, the fault is your own.' And this was just. The training had been full and fair.

'But now,' I said, ' I must sleep.'

A long succession of thoughts moved with leaden feet across my mind, some startling me, so that my heart pounded alarmingly. Sometimes the succession quickened, flitting like something living across my closed eyes. At last I said, 'What is it that's worrying you? Face it out, then go to sleep. Is it that tomorrow night you might die? What of that? Death is life's only certainty. The only difference in this life is that we know approximately when it will strike.'

I turned over to sleep, facing the inert figure of Harry. His position was unchanged. He might have been sleeping in Brisbane, in his bed at home.

I was becoming drowsy when I heard aircraft circling overhead. These, I knew, would be the night flying crews returning to base. Tomorrow we would be using the same 'planes, while these crews would stand aside, regarding us open-mouthed and wondering. I had not slept when they walked by for breakfast. They walked quietly, talking in subdued voices. The window above our beds grew slowly pale...

At 6.30, half an hour before the others, I rose and went to the washroom. I had the absurd idea that fear and weariness must be so clearly stamped on my face that all the world could see them, and that if I showered perhaps they would vanish. But as I shaved I was surprised that the face confronting me was unchanged.

We were briefed in the late afternoon. In our crew sat Vin Givney, an enthusiastic young Australian bomb aimer borrowed to replace Ted. The doors were closed and in a slightly theatrical manner an intelligence officer made the announcement we were waiting to hear.

'The target for tonight,' he said, 'is Bremen.'

As he paused I heard a sound like distant surf from the men about me.

'Would someone draw the blinds, please?'

I glanced out at a blue sky, with a light bank of cloud to the west, before the room was darkened. Bremen; just where was Bremen? My geography of Germany was hopeless. What had the instructors said about it? Was it 'good' or 'bad'?

An aerial photograph was projected on to the screen. Near the centre of it was a red spot.

'This, gentlemen, is Bremen, the second port of Germany.' He pointed then to the red spot. 'This is your aiming point.'

I looked closely at the clustered buildings and the maze of streets, the scene being so deliberately set for the night's holocaust. The men were silent. Beside me I heard Geoff breathing and from the light of the epidiascope saw his eyes fixed on the screen. On the far side of him were other men, motionless and staring. There was something ugly in the room; something grotesque. However much one may read of war and train for war; it is not until the unbelievable moments before action that reality suddenly strangles one. We were about to kill people we had never seen. And they would attempt to kill us. I felt an urgent need to think, even though I knew that all my thinking of the past three years had failed to clarify my mind. To kill. Let me see this clearly. To kill and to be killed. Why was this, again? Freedom; yes, that was it; for freedom. Whose freedom? Freedom for what?

The intelligence officer's conclusion caught my attention. '— to break the morale of the workers.'

I felt the pressure of Geoff's elbow. 'Better copy down some of the Met. gen.'

Before us now there was a weather chart. The met man was reading the forecast. Over Europe there was low cloud and rain, but at operating level, clear skies. On our return there would probably be fog over East Anglia, but the south should remain clear.

When he had finished, the blinds were raised and daylight filled the room. The sky beyond the windows had faded and along the nearby path men not concerned with the flap were walking to the mess. Rosevear, the Senior Navigation Officer, was twisting a strand of wool about a number of pins in a map of Europe, each pin marking a turning-point in our route. The sight of him was somehow reassuring. In the flap of our departure, he was one of the few who appeared unconfused by operational procedure. He was a shortish, solid navigator, who always addressed us with an interested inclination of the head and enquiring eyes. I once heard someone remark that he looked and walked like a farmer. Although a Squadron Leader, he wore the highly valued ribbon of the DFM.

'Navigators, I will give you your route. Base to Cromer, Cromer to Enkhuisen — E-n-k-h-u-i-s-e-n, here on the Zuider Zee; Enkhuisen to position 52°50'N 8°40'E, then a short run to the target.'

So typical was the route of the theoretical plots we had done for the past year, that I began to feel we might even yet go to another room and make one more simulated attack.

'Take-off is at 2315; time on target 0200.'

The Wing Commander came to the edge of the platform. He was thin and dark and often scathing in his speech.

'The crew that came in late for briefing, have you got everything down? You have? All right, then. When you come in late like that, salute as you enter the room — and don't look as if you were about to enter the Valley of the Shadow.'

It appeared that a large force was to bomb the target between 1.0 and 1.30am. There was then to be a misleading lull until we attacked at 2.0. We were to fly at 9,000ft. This, the Wing Commander assured us, was 'the best height to fly — too high for the light flak and too low for the heavy flak and night fighters.' In truth, it was a bad height for everything.

'You will report to your flights at 2200 hours.' The Wing Commander paused. 'Any questions? None? Very well, you will each file past this table and the intelligence officer will issue you with escape equipment.'

In another room the navigators drew tracks to Bremen on Mercator charts. Keith Webber stood beside me, checking and rechecking each bearing with his protractor. Behind us Harry Wright whistled tunelessly but contentedly. In the company of these two men I was to see much. On this day they were equals; equal, I think, in intelligence and courage; equal in training. Equal in everything except luck, or fate, or destiny. I walked with them back to the mess, facing the tranquil spires of Lichfield in a sky now cloudless and already darkening.

Our meal was late. We rushed through the first course, then went directly to the flight office. By now it was dark and brilliant with stars. In the flight office the navigators were spreading their logs and charts on a table that ran the length of the room. I settled next to Joe Turnbull, the oldest of the Twenty Men. He was rubicund and vociferous and might easily have passed as a bookmaker, or perhaps a stage comedian. Joe had always professed to believe himself insufficiently intelligent to become a navigator.

'Listen, boy, I'm laying odds of five to two that I'm scrubbed after the next tests. They should have made me a gunner in the first place. Five to two! Any takers?'

No one ever took him seriously, but his success would have been a safe bet, for he always got through. We had begun to discuss the forecast winds when an agitated Flight Sergeant ran in.

'Is Turnbull here?'

'Yes!'

'You should be over at C Flight. All your crew are waiting for you.'

'Tell them to come over here. I've got my stuff spread out on the table.'

'Now, listen, Turnbull, don't start an argument at this stage.'

I noticed that the Flight Sergeant was smiling. Evidently he knew Joe from past experience. But Joe picked up his belongings, grumbling, and walked out.

Outside the moon was up, shining horizontally across the top of darkened trees. The night was ominously calm. Geoff sniffed the air as we walked to our bus.

'There'll be a fog, all right. They'll probably divert us to the other end of the country.'

In the dark interior of the bus a sudden paralysis gripped me. I was a man in a dream who wanted to run away, but who was rooted to where he stood. This feeling remained with me in the aircraft. I looked incredulously about the cabin, at the desk and the chart, much as a man might look at the block in the moment before his execution. It was impossible! There were issues I needed to understand. But the engines had been started and we moved away.

Max Bryant watched us from the edge of the aerodrome, as I had watched the ops take-off on my first night at Lichfield. That night he wrote in his diary:

'I saw them go off — one up, two up, three up. They came thundering up the runway, lumbering heavily, lifting off at the end. At about 2350, with two crates still to take off, a terrible thing happened. There was a yell from control, "Stand by ambulance and fire wagon — aircraft coming in with port engine afire." There was silence for a few minutes, then Davies' voice, "Get ready to move."'

'Towards the end of the runway I could see the green light on the starboard wing as the crate came in. He seemed to do a steep turn on his one engine, then suddenly the light dashed straight into the ground. There was a loud crash and immediately a great cloud of flame burst into the air. I heard Davies yell, "There are bombs on that aircraft. Get the others in the air immediately!" The flames were leaping skyward and there were bright flashes and explosions as flares and ammunition blew up.'

'By now I had discovered that the navigator was poor old Joe Turnbull. For a few moments I felt sick and shaken; only after a while did I realize that the crew would never know what hit them.'

'At about 2400 hours there was a terrific explosion which shook the huts. Later there was another explosion as the rest of the bombs went. In this, four of the ground crew lost their lives.'

'Nine men gone in a short few minutes and one of them the first of the Twenty. I crawled to bed and prayed in cowardly manner that I might not die as Joe had done.'

And so the men who had been late for briefing passed through the Valley. By us the crash had not been seen. We were climbing towards the Norfolk coast over a floor of cloud, white in the moonlight. Near the coast the cloud broke, revealing Wroxham, 15 miles south of track. I checked the wind and altered course for Enkhuisen, doing my only worthwhile navigation for the journey. Below us, unclouded but dark, lay the North Sea.

'We have left England,' I thought, 'and are headed for the enemy coast. We have left those places where people sit in comparative security and talk and read of war, and we are being rushed into actualities.'

'Navigator, height nine thousand feet. Oxygen on, please.'

I left the warmth of the cabin, closing the door behind me. In the belly of the 'plane the roar of the engines and the outer rush of the slipstream were intensified. The rows of oxygen bottles in their racks over my head were cold to the touch. Standing there I felt an almost physical wave of fear and rebellion. Why were we in this inhospitable sky, hurtling towards that long-dreaded line, the enemy coast? Why should we kill and be killed? What was it about, this appalling slaughter? But I switched on my microphone and heard my own detached, casual voice in my ears, 'Oxygen on, Geoff.'

'Thanks, navigator. If you can spare a moment, see if you can spot anything from the astro-dome.'

In the astro-dome the illusion of protection offered by the fuselage was lost. The night was mild and clear, but, looking to all sides, I could see nothing, nothing but shadows here and there deeper than the rest. Above the dust and smoke of the earth, the stars appeared bigger and more brilliant, their twinkling a visible throbbing. A thousand airmen's eyes were watching them as I watched them and I wondered if to all those other men they seemed so supremely indifferent, so baffling in their permanence.

Geoff's voice said in my ears, 'I can see some sort of light ahead. I'll start weaving.'

As I peered ahead, the starboard wing dipped and we dived slowly. I saw the light Geoff had mentioned, a vague, moving light, like a searchlight on clouds. We levelled out and began to climb; twisted then to port. The light grew clearer. Somewhere below it a soundless explosion lit the sky ahead.

Geoff spoke again. 'I think a kite went in.'

It was the first 'plane we had seen shot down, but it was so far away that instead of my fears increasing they began to slip away.

A new excitement enveloped me. We were entering a game in which skill and luck were combined; the stakes were our lives. Now we must watch; especially we must watch below.

I glanced down as we banked again to port. 'I can see moonlight faintly on the sea.'

'Yes, I saw it a moment ago. I think I can see a ship, too. Bomb aimer, look down to starboard. Isn't that — Hell!'

An explosion obliterated the voices and I found myself lying across the mainspar.

Then Geoff's voice. 'Turning port!'

I groped back to my table. Max Burcher, who had heard none of the conversation, looked at me eagerly. I slipped off my mask and stooped over him.

'A flak ship — put a shot just below us!'

His eyes dilated. 'Where are we?'

'Just coming to the Dutch coast. I'd better check up.'

'OK. I'll take your place in the astro-dome.'

He picked up an empty bottle and waved it gleefully.

'Supposed to put out the searchlights if you chuck it out.'

He went back into the darkness, leaving me to the chart. On it were our tracks; a couple of fixes and, over Europe, blotches of red marked there during the afternoon. These were the heavily defended areas.

'Navigator from bomb aimer: searchlights and flak on our starboard bow.'

With little confidence I replied, 'Amsterdam.'

Silence fell again. I opened the forward door and looked past the indistinct silhouette of Geoff into the darkness ahead. It was as the instructors had said — gun flashes, moving searchlights and sudden explosions. For a time I thought the explosions were caused by our men bombing in some sort of diversionary raid, but gradually I realized that each explosion came from an aircraft crashing to the ground. I looked again at Geoff's back. There was something reassuring about it, as though through him we would remain indestructible. Somewhere beyond him were 'They' whose work it was to kill us before we killed them. Over us all rose the indifferent stars, climbing from east to west. Orion's Belt stood low before us.

'Navigator from bomb aimer: we're coming up to a straight sort of coast. There's a light flashing to starboard and another one a good way off to port.'

'Thanks.'

I saw from the chart that there were lighthouses both to port and starboard of our track, but then there appeared to be lighthouses marked all the way from the Friesians to the

Belgian border. We could conceivably be between any two of them. But within some minutes Vin Givney spoke again. 'I believe we're coming up to Enkhuisen. I can see moonlight on water not far ahead.' He paused. I could feel him staring into the darkness. 'Yes, Enkhuisen just ahead. I'll tell you when we're over it, navigator. Coming up —coming up — now!'

I checked the wind and altered course for Bremen, then changed places with Max Burcher.

As we groped past in the darkness, I felt the cold fabric of his flying suit against my hand.

'Where are we now?'

'Crossing the Zuider Zee — about forty minutes from the target.'

'Fine! I'll listen out to base and change over with you later.'

He clambered over the mainspar, leaving me alone with the roar of the engines and the stars. There was still confused activity on the coast behind us, but immediately about us the night was quiet. Looking out into the darkness, I was slowly lulled into a feeling of security.

As we came to the far shore ten or twelve searchlights reached into the sky off our port quarter. They formed a cone, and in the apex of the cone the sky was suddenly blotched with soundless, reddish explosions. Both the cone and the shell bursts moved our way.

I heard myself say to Geoff, 'Searchlights and flak to port.'

But even as he climbed and twisted to escape them, I felt the whole scene to be unreal. That there were men down there I could not believe. Rather, in that listening darkness, there was one vast animal-machine, its tentacles these frenzied beams.

A beam swung across the sky close behind us. 'Shag' muttered huskily, 'Searchlight dead astern.'

His voice sounded indignant, as though he had a personal grudge against those below. Geoff redoubled his weaving.

As we passed beyond their reach the searchlights went out; not singly, but together, as though governed by a single mind which was waiting now for those behind us. Below us there was now no light of any kind; above, only the stars. Orion was higher in the east, Polaris high on our port beam. For sound there was only the song of the engines.

I tried to tell myself that below in the darkness there were people, in their ears the drone of engines that was in my own. But even as I tried to visualize them, these people were unreal and, throughout my operational life, were to remain so.

A shadow sped past us, blacker than the night.

'Single-engined fighter just passed — don't think 'e saw us.'

The port wing dipped; the starboard wing pointed skyward. The moon glistened on their dewy surfaces. Max Burcher climbed over the mainspar again.

'Ready for a change over?'

I edged past him and returned to my neglected chart.

'How long before we reach the target?'

'About fifteen minutes.'

I gave Geoff this time with little hope that it would prove correct. We had had no sort of check since leaving the Zuider Zee, and tonight I was capable of only the most elementary navigation. Whether it would be wise or not to ask Geoff to stop his weaving while I took star shots, or while Max tried for radio bearings, I did not know. I realized, then, why it was that a man's first five operations were all-important. If he survived them, he was beginning to have some idea of operational technique. As we were this night I had none.

'I can see a dull red glow through the clouds ahead,' said Geoff slowly. 'It looks almost certain to be the target. What would you say, bomb aimer?'

'Yes; yes, I would say that that's Bremen all right. It's a good way off yet but sometimes you can see a sudden flash like a bomb burst.'

I opened the forward door to see for myself. Geoff was

now plainly silhouetted against a reddened sky perhaps thirty miles away. Faintly against the glare I could see the beams of searchlights, moving restlessly. In that moment my fear of the target suddenly vanished in the relief of finding it. I went back to check the time.

'We're due on the target in eight minutes.'

'Thanks. I don't think I'll be hanging round this place longer than necessary.'

As Geoff answered me he turned slightly starboard, already seeking a gap in the defences. His turn brought the target within sight of the rear turret. An exclamation burst from 'Shag'.

'Gawd! We're not going in there, are we? Think of my missus!'

We laughed, but no one made further comment. I looked at the commonplace things on my desk — pencils, a scribbling block, a pear ripened in the Staffordshire sun — and suddenly I thought of them as wonderfully sane, inanimate though they were. Just beyond them, death grasped at our fabric walls.

'Flak and searchlights ahead — bags of them!'

Light flak was rising as though from the nozzles of ten thousand hoses, forming transient, erratic patterns in red and green and yellow. Above it the heavy flak blotched the sky with red, and left greyish puffs of smoke drifting on the wind. Shining through this inferno were searchlights, threshing this way and that, sometimes finding an aircraft, sometimes losing one. The whole picture was silent, like a piece of fantastic photography on a silent screen. The only sound in our ears was the endless throb of the engines. 'Taffy', our Welsh navigation instructor, had once said, 'Dawn't be shaken by the target and give a wrong course hawm. There was a navigator once who gave the pilot the ground speed to steer instead of the course and it took them right into the Ruhr.'

Remembering this navigator, I went back to the illusory safety of the cabin.

Finally Geoff spoke. He reminded me of a diver poised on a high board, summoning up courage for the plunge.

'OK, here we go!'

His voice was subdued. I thought that there was an unusual note in it of regret, or sadness, strange in such a place. The nose of the Wellington dropped and the roar of the engines slackened. No one was speaking, but somewhere a piece of loose fabric was flapping angrily. The forward door fell open, revealing a sight beyond description. That men could pass through such a place and live was unbelievable. We passed tall columns of searchlights that groped and missed, sometimes filling the cockpit with blue glare. Down; down. The light flak was now a moving carpet.

'I see the aiming point, Skipper.'

'Tell me when you're ready.'

A shell burst close by, shattering the illusion of silence and bringing an odour of cordite into the cabin. No one spoke.

'OK, Skipper, steady up. Bomb doors open.'

'Bomb doors open.'

For twenty years we hung suspended, the streams of red and yellow flicking by. I could feel the updraught of air through the bomb doors and hear the flapping fabric.

The 'plane leapt upward.

'Bombs gone!'

I wrote in my log, '0206 Bombs gone.'

'Course out, navigator?'

I passed it quickly and Geoff went into a steep turn. We were battling through the searchlights from the inside. The bursting of shells had intensified, sounding like the barking of mammoth dogs below our fuselage. A searchlight lit the cabin weirdly, slipped on to the wing, then was gone. Suddenly we were out. Darkness was again below us, only the stars above. For a long time no one spoke, then I heard Geoff. 'What time do we reach the English coast?'

'Five o'clock,' I said.

'Nearly three bloody hours!'

Far ahead and to port we could see the flak and

searchlights of the Ruhr. When we had passed it I did not leave my chair, but sagged there, staring at the dazzling chart, watching our slow progress over its white expanse. Sometimes I felt that we were no longer moving; that we had become one with the planets and would never land.

Darkness; searchlights and bursts of flak; sudden attacks by fighters and the hoarse cries of the gunners; darkness again and the stars. A thousand tons of harness about our necks; the roar of engines …

'It's breaking dawn, navigator, and we're coming up to the Dutch coast.'

At the voice I started and answered confusedly, 'OK, thanks. Let's know when we cross.'

I was fighting sleep when the bomb aimer answered again.

'Over it now, navigator, pretty well on track.'

Half an hour dragged by. The first sun shone in the rear gunner's face and revealed the North Sea below, limitless and innocent.

After a long time the bomb aimer spoke again.

'There's a bank of fog lying on the sea ahead. I think it follows the English coast.'

'Where do you reckon we are?' asked Geoff.

'We should be approaching Cromer,' I said, 'but I think we're further south. Max is getting a bearing.'

But Max had been interrupted. He handed me a slip of paper on which were two words, DIVERTED TEMPSFORD.

'Where is it?'

He shook his head. 'Never heard of it.'

I repeated the message to Geoff.

'Do you know where it is?'

'I think it's near Cambridge,' he said. 'Anyway, you'd better find out damn' quickly — we haven't much gas left.'

Below us the fog lay in a grey blanket to every horizon. I unfolded the map of the Cambridge area and began searching for Tempsford. Through smarting eyes I saw

Mildenhall, Oakington, Watton; but of Tempsford not a sign.

'Listen, navigator, we've got to do something pretty smartly. We've only enough fuel——'

'Bomb aimer to navigator: the fog here is breaking and I can see a beacon.'

I grasped the list of characteristics. 'It's flashing MP.'

By some strange good fortune, MP was Tempsford.

We plunged through the breaking fog, calling control for instructions. In a moment we trundled to a dispersal and had our last words with control. The song of the engines ceased. Geoff opened the forward door, letting light and air drive the last remnants of night from our cabin. I stood up stiffly and through puckered eyes saw a quiet, grey dawn. Operation number one was over and an endless week in Scotland lay before me.

Our coming into Glen Urquhart I have always remembered. Though the country was different from any I had seen, I felt strangely reminded of my pre-war home. On our hills hundreds of sheep had grazed and the sound of them had been with us always. As we entered Glen Urquhart the same sound met us, the bleating of sheep up and down the hills on the evening air.

I was walking with two of the Twenty Men: Harry Waddell, whom I had once dubbed the 'Cheerful Pessimist', and George Loder, the 'Imperturbable.' Harry was a plump, pink-cheeked fellow who flogged his apparently soft body with violent exercise. He had the disconcerting habit of declaring that our chances of survival were negligible and then of laughing at his prediction uproariously. George, on the other hand, gave no hint of his expectations. When action came I felt that he would go to meet it with the same quiet determination with which he handled problems in class. It was a challenge and, though it swept him away, it would not deter him. I did not know for a long time that he had a baby daughter whom he had never seen. Harry only knew of this because the two had been friends before the war. Their friendship now was near its end.

We had walked this day from Inverness, 20 bituminous miles, when we had foolishly hoped for rough bridle paths. But, for me, Loch Ness and the company of George and Harry had saved the day. Harry walked with the same tremendous gusto that he put into all things. Either he swung his arms like a drill sergeant and glared at the horizon, or he clasped his hands behind his back and stared at the road, cogitating over some absurd argument. Slung round his neck was his Leica, which swung loosely as he walked. His pack was bigger than George's and mine, being crammed with photographic gear and everything he could carry that might make the journey a more comfortable one.

George's walk was more relaxed. Whereas Harry leaned aggressively forward, George walked erect, his calm, level eyes seldom changing in expression. Occasionally an amused smile played about his mouth as he listened to Harry put forward one of his preposterous arguments. Of us all, he was the most complete man. He had poise, quiet dignity and was master of his emotions.

Our road turned slowly westward, leaving the main sheet of Loch Ness behind and following the narrow water of Glen Urquhart. On our other side a hill rose to a dominating crest. The crest was lost in a dense wood, but fields on the lower slopes were being ploughed as we passed. We heard the faint cries of the ploughmen urging their horses. Behind them seagulls wheeled and screamed and sometimes settled, white on the chocolate furrows.

Further on we came to the war memorial of Drumnadrochit. On it were the names of eight McDonalds and several Frasers and the words, 'Ladich a Chlinne a Thuit San Arach'. This was translated, 'They Rose and Fell that Right might Prevail.' Close by was our inn …

When our journey was near its end and we stood on the summit of Ben Nevis with half Scotland at our feet, George said, 'We must come here again.'

Harry laughed, leaving us unprepared for his answer.

'You don't imagine you'll see another leave, do you?'

His belief was well founded. He was lost on operations shortly after. But George's end was still far off.

CHAPTER FOUR

Posting to Elsham Wolds

N ear each squadron aerodrome there was usually a small village which was also the aerodrome's nearest railhead. These wayside stations were the first thing a new arrival saw and, if he survived, they were the last thing he saw as he departed. When he was setting out on leave, or going for an evening off camp, he would see the station as a gateway to the gaiety of London or Lincoln. It would beckon him with its promise of escape to places where time did not exist. But when he returned he would see the same station darkly, as a gateway to fear and tension.

Such a station was Barnetby Junction, the nearest railhead to Elsham Wolds. Like most of the aerodrome villages, Barnetby had been lifted from obscurity by the war and gave the impression that after the RAF had passed by it would lapse into obscurity again.

Very clearly I can see us there, the men of four newly arrived crews — Laing's crew, Cook's crew, Bayliss's crew and Maddern's crew, which last was my own. We were twenty men in all, but of our twenty only eight were destined to depart from Barnetby station a few months later. And as it was with our crews, so it was with scores of others. Twenty sergeants, we stood on the platform looking up at hills that rose gently on every side, wondering vaguely in what direction lay our new station. Two Halifaxes were droning across the sky, drifting heavily to port in a strong wind. As we watched their crabbing motion, I wondered with a start whether I would always be successful in detecting such drift as this in the nights over Germany. To fail to allow for it, or to allow for it incorrectly, could prove disastrous. I glanced at the men about me, finding reassurance in their company.

After an hour at Barnetby a van arrived from Elsham. We loaded our belongings into it and for the first time travelled the road that was to imprint itself on the minds of each of us. Uphill it led to comradeship, fear and death; downhill to relief, safety and, I think, to loneliness. It rose out of the valley of Barnetby; it passed the last farms and the Elsham Waafery and a wood where the leaves had turned to gold. It crossed a main road at right-angles. Beyond this point, which was called the Barnetby crossroads, the way levelled considerably. About us were undulating fields very much open to the wind. In some of them sugar beet grew; in others stood haystacks, surrounded by the stubble of crops harvested not long before. Occasionally the road dipped, but the greater part of the journey lay uphill until, at another and minor crossroad, we turned left and faced the highest part of the wolds. There, against the sky, we could see the level expanse of an aerodrome. Beside the aerodrome rose the bulk of hangars; a glass-fronted watch office; a tall water tower and other lower buildings clustered about them.

As we drew closer we could see Halifaxes dispersed about the rim of the landing field. Presently we could read their squadron identification painted in dull red on their black sides, PM. At various points about the perimeter white windsocks swung rigidly in the strong wind. On the watch office roof the cups of the anemometer whirled unceasingly. These things, huddled under a moody sky, were the home of 103 Squadron. If the squadron averaged twenty crews of seven men each, and if the ratio of ground crew to air crew was ten to one, as we were told it was, then the population of Elsham Wolds must have been over 1,500 men.

We had imagined a squadron to be a place different from anything we had previously known. Perhaps in our hearts we had expected a place in which highly efficient men lived against a background fitting the drama of their lives, rather as a battleship is a fitting background to the life of her crew. All through our long training we had coloured and dramatized the squadron picture. At Elsham came our disillusioning. In the usual way we visited the Sick Quarters for a quick examination; were issued with blankets; were cursed hoarsely by a Flight Sergeant and, finally, were shown into a long, low-ceilinged hut, no different from the huts of Lichfield.

This but was already partly occupied by a few operational men. There was Ben Hardisty, a Canadian; Andy Stubbs, an Australian; a Scot named Porter, beside whom I was to sleep, and a particularly coarse but good-natured Australian known to everyone as 'Bull'.

Hardisty flew with Porter, the soft-voiced Scot. Above Porter's bed was a photograph of a girl.

'We're to be married at Christmas,' he told me.

Andy Stubbs was short and dark and permanently cheerful. About his neatness and the friendly cock of his head there was something that reminded me strongly of a bird.

'Bull' was built like a bull; he had the voice of a bull and the instincts of a bull. He came in while we were making our beds and roared in a voice that shook the barracks, 'Just had a lovely naughty! What a girl!'

He came down to his bed.

'How's my oppo Stubbs?'

Andy faced him firmly.

'Now listen, "Bull", let's get to bed. Tomorrow night we'll probably be on ops.'

At this 'Bull' looked thoughtful.

'Bloody silly life, isn't it? Who the hell wants to have flak pumped at them?'

Receiving no answer, he undressed and went to bed.

In the morning the men prepared for operations, as Andy had predicted. We, the newcomers, began our conversion to Halifaxes. We reported to a pale, boyish Squadron Leader, who wore the ribbons of the DSO and DFC over his battle dress pocket. Of his words I remember very little, but his dark, staring eyes I have never forgotten. I felt that they had looked on the worst; and on looking beyond it, had found serenity. They gazed from an impassive face with a challengingly upthrust chin and a firm mouth.

This was David Halford, one of the most striking men we met in the RAF. He had won the DFC, it was said, at eighteen and the DSO at twenty-one and now, at twenty-two, had recently finished his second tour — at this time a total of sixty operations. A year later, when Halford was Wing Commander at Lindholme, I heard a Flight Sergeant say that if he returned for a third tour half Lindholme would want to follow him. Eventually Halford did return. Then, one foggy night as he came in to land, he crashed and was killed. That was in 1943 but as we saw him now, on our first morning at Elsham, he was the personification of all that was best in the RAF.

In the mess during morning tea we were among the ops men again. What we had expected of the mess on an operational station I don't quite know — perhaps a gathering of aloof, highly-decorated men in a chilly atmosphere. We found the opposite. In the mess anything could happen. Bike races occurred; men left footprints on the ceiling; the piano was plied with beer by grateful singers; the furniture was turned upside down so that aircrew men could fling themselves over it.

At morning tea this day a story was going the rounds.

'So the Wingco goes to the Kirmington party. There he is, blind as a bloody newt, and what do they do? Whip his bags off! Send him home in his underpants!'

The sequel to this came shortly before lunch. A Wellington flew low overhead; a parachute appeared and, suspended from it, the Wing Commander's trousers. The Wing Commander, we heard, took a poor view. Someone or other at Kirmington was going to be posted.

'What a black! What a bloody black!'

It did not take long to find that the lives of squadron men hinged on the day's announcement of ops. If there were no ops they either had a do in the mess, or bolted post haste for Scunthorpe, in crews or with girl friends. What they did in Scunthorpe no one much cared. They had one obligation — to be fit for operations the moment they were required.

By four o'clock the high spirits of the ops men had subsided. Briefing was over and only we of the Conversion Unit were allowed off the camp. A friend had given me a Cleethorpes address, so that night I went to it. I went diffidently, but I left next morning knowing I had a home whenever I wished to go to it.

In the morning, before daylight, I returned to Cleethorpes station. The town was empty and very cold, a fitful wind blowing through the streets. In the sky, the Plough was twisted into a position strange to me. How well I remember the third-class LNER compartment in which I sat that morning and on all those mornings that were to follow! The closed windows misted by ten breaths; the smell of dusty seats and stale cigarette smoke; the heavy-booted Lincolnshire workmen setting out for the city of 'Ool; or for work on the aerodromes of Kirmin't'n, or Grimsby, or half a dozen others. If ever I return to Lincolnshire and see and hear and smell these things again, even after twenty years, a chill will enter my heart. I shall rub the misted windows and look out at the sunrise, the thought in my mind, 'It's going to be fine. Ops tonight are certain.'

By the time we reached Barnetby it was full light. Fifteen or twenty heavily-clad girls stepped off the train and, with coarse remarks in thick Lincolnshire accents, they boarded a truck for the beet fields on the wolds. I walked up the hill to the Barnetby crossroads, past the Waafery and past the last farm. The morning was cold and still, the sun shining horizontally across mist-wreathed fields and hedges.

When I reached the camp many of the men were rising, but in our own barracks there was darkness and silence. The smell of last night's fire, of dirty clothes and unwashed bodies, met me at the door. RAF gunners were asleep in shirts that appeared welded to their bodies by the dirt of weeks. At Harry Wright's bed I stopped. All to be seen of Harry was the top of his unruly head. I stooped over him.

'Out you come, Wright!'

'Ssh!'

He poked his head from the blankets, like a tortoise from its shell.

'Aachen.'

I looked towards the ops men's beds.

'Are they all back?'

'I don't know. They came in late.'

I went to my bed, but before I reached it I saw that both Porter's bed and Hardisty's were empty. Opposite me Andy Stubbs was already awake, but silent.

'No word of them?'

He shook his head and lay staring at the ceiling. 'Bull' was awake too. The roar had gone from his voice. With determined indifference he said, 'That's the way it goes, son; that's the way it goes.'

The girl's photograph still· stood over Porter's bed, looking out with the same gentle eyes. Hardisty's things were neatly arranged at the head of his bed. I recalled his words of twenty-four hours before, 'I sure never wanted to come to 103 Squadron.'

As I stood there between the two beds, a feeling of desperation seized me. That we could go on like this was unthinkable. Someone must stop the whole insane business. Porter and Hardisty were dead! I went to the mess vaguely expecting rebelliousness or sadness or anger, but found only a mask of indifference and did not even recognize it as a mask.

Operations were on again. We saw the crews at lunch time crowding about the coke stoves in the mess. Outside the day was cold. A wind from the North Sea drove evil-looking clouds before it and flung rain against the windows. In the woods near the barracks the first leaves were being torn from the trees and scattered along muddy pathways. The men about the stoves were talking quietly among themselves.

'They might scrub it.'

'It'll take more than this.'

'You might be right. Anyway, dirty nights are better in a

way. You don't see so much of their fighters.'

'Wonder if that's what got Porter?'

'Wouldn't be surprised.'

The opening of the dining room broke the conversation.

At 3pm a padlocked wire encircled the 'phone box, preventing outward calls. In the mess the crews began appearing wearing heavy white sweaters beneath their battle dress, as Porter and Hardisty had done the night before. The weather outside had worsened. Darkness was coming rapidly, hastened by low cloud and unceasing rain. On the sports ground seagulls were alighting, driven inland by storms.

Having eaten before us, the ops crews left the mess. They had become quiet and unsmiling. By the time we had eaten tea it was dusk. I walked through the rain towards our hut, past the sports ground and the cabbage field to the restless, disconsolate wood. The Halifaxes were starting up, filling the evening with wind-tossed roarings. Our hut was empty. When I reached its further end I saw that Porter's and Hardisty's kits had gone. Their beds were iron frames waiting for new tenants.

I lay on my bed, thinking involuntarily of a man our instructor had spoken of that day. Over the target he had screamed. He was ashamed and apologetic, but they had taken him off ops immediately. What would become of him? Probably, we were told, he would be classed as 'lacking in moral fibre'. Though the thought of him was vaguely troubling, I fell asleep. I must have slept some little time, when I dreamed that I wakened and saw Porter lying asleep on the next bed. The shock roused me completely. Someone was running into the barracks, stamping the mud from his feet at the door. Looking up, I saw that it was 'Bull', the rain streaming off his cape.

'Ops are scrubbed, son! There we were, sitting in the kites, when they told us. They're putting on an extra bus for Scunthorpe, so tonight I get drunk. No popsies tonight; I just get drunk.'

This was accepted ritual following loss of friends.

The men came trooping in noisily, the masks off their faces. They began changing into best blues, singing and shouting continually. I wondered whether to go to the mess to see if any of our crew would join the exodus, but the bus was almost due to leave. I changed quickly and joined the crews.

The first bus pulled up at our door with a shriek of brakes. As we clambered in at the back, hurrying to get out of the rain, a dim blue light was switched on. It blanched the faces of twenty or thirty men who had begun singing with steaming breaths:

'They say there's a Lancaster leaving Berlin
Bound for old Blighty's shore,
Heavily laden with terrified men
Bound for the land they adore.'

The light was switched out, but the singing continued as we sped through the gates and down the road. At the Barnetby crossroads we stopped and a dozen rain-soaked Waafs were helped in at the back. This was the last stop. When the blue light had been switched off, we raced madly for Scunthorpe through wet, invisible countryside, our tyres hissing on the roads. Except for the glow of cigarettes and the occasional flare of a match, we rode in darkness, a darkness loud with singing.

Scunthorpe was unknown to me, but it was the town most patronized by the Elsham men. There one could get drunk at the 'Crosby', or see a floor show and get drunk at the 'Oswald', or dance and get drunk at the 'Berkley'. And in the event of missing the bus back, it was always possible to stay the night at Irish Maggie's and return to camp by train in the morning. In my memory Scunthorpe is blacked out and wet, for only in poor weather did we escape to it. So often did I find my way about it in darkness, that its streets and buildings became places built in my imagination, rather than the streets and buildings of actuality.

We pulled up in a side street of unrelieved blackness. As the noise of the engine ceased I heard the rain pelting still on the roof and then a cry from several throats, 'Everybody out!' the blue light was switched on and I found that Keith Webber had been sitting only a few men away from me. He smiled as he saw me. 'Thought I might go to the "Berkley". The boys say the dances there are quite good.'

'Do you mind if I join you?'

'Of course not.'

We stumbled through the darkness to a faintly lighted taxi, which took us to a building on the outskirts of the town. Somewhere inside, an orchestra throbbed a tango. We stepped out of the rain and darkness into the sudden brilliance of a large dance floor. RAF men, Poles, Americans, Canadians and Australians circled and swayed under a pall of tobacco smoke. The orchestra was playing 'Jealousy', a tango interwoven with our Elsham lives.

Of that evening in Scunthorpe there is little I remember, except a first glimpse of Joan Sutherland. We had been in the room for some time when I saw her, standing among a group of Waafs. Her figure and the way in which she held herself gave her the appearance of being tall, though I could see from those about her that she was of no more than medium height. To conform to WAAF regulations, her fair hair was combed upward away from her collar in a way that suited her well. I noticed that her eyes were animated and gay while she was speaking to others, but in repose, grave and almost lonely. Several times I was about to ask her to dance, but something about her discouraged quick acquaintance and each time my courage failed me. She left early, and though I saw her often about Elsham in the weeks ahead, we did not meet for nearly three months.

At 10pm Keith and I found our way to the buses. The first one was drawing away, leaving a crowd of singing latecomers lurching through the rain. They packed the second bus to suffocation, scrambling in without a pause in their discordant singing. Keith and I became separated, he being pushed somewhere forward among the mass of bodies and I being left against the back. The bus started with a lurch and the singing increased in volume. Sometimes three or four different songs were being sung together; the most tuneless now shouted to the skies.

The song being sung by the majority rose to greater volume.

'She's a great big dame,
Twice the size of me,
With hairs on her belly
Like the branches on a tree.'

With each expulsion of the singers' breaths, the smell of regurgitated beer became stronger. Sometimes I swayed into the clear air outside, but as we rounded each bend I fell inward against a shadowy Waaf, absorbed in conversation with a gunner.

'I kep' thinking we'd had it. Then right in fron' of us, a Hallie blew up. I keep won'ering if was 'ole Porter - '

'Salome! Salome!
She's my girl Salome!
Standing there - '

'It's these damn' kites. There's something wrong with the rudder. Not a crew's got through on them, not a damn' crew.'

'But you'll come through; I know you'll come through.'

'It's no good kidding yoursel', Meg. My skipper reckons they'll keep ge'ing these losses 'slong's they doan - '

I swung out again into the night. The tail light gleamed faintly on the wet road. The tyres hissed loudly. Black trees occasionally swished by, almost touching our sides. The singing in the hot interior had become a roar with something bitter in it.

'Singing hi! Jimmy, ho! Jimmy,
Come along with me,
Singing hi! Jimmy, ho! Jimmy Johnson.'

The chorus ended and the solo part was sung by the tenor. Assisting him were two or three semi-conscious choristers, one of whom was singing 'Trees' under some misapprehension. The air by now had been replaced by beer fumes, cigarette smoke, Waafs' perfume and an odour of wet coats. To this was added a new odour, penetrating and alarming. There were cries of, 'Man sick! Let him get to the back!' Then, 'Damn' you! Sick on my hand! Can't you get by me?'

The vomiting man was moving slowly to the end of the bus.

'Oh, Chrish', lemme reash the back!'

The song had reached the solo part again.

'Cats on the roof tops
Cats on the tiles - '
'A tree ooz 'ungry mouth is pres-st
Againsht th' -'

I swayed again into the night. The rain was passing, leaving clear skies to the west. Ops tomorrow would be a certainty. At my side the sick man vomited on to the road. Sometimes he gasped 'Poor bloody Hardisty' and 'Oh, Chrish', I shouldna got drunk.'

His cap fell on to the road. We shouted to the driver but the bus swayed on. The song reached its lowest levels, then ceased. In the comparative silence a falsetto rose like the voice of a choirboy.

'Jesus wants me for a sunbeam.'

The drunk and the sober yelled the response,

'And a bloody fine sunbeam am I!'

The Waaf was speaking urgently. 'No, Johnnie, no, you've been drinking.'

'But I'm no' drunk, Meg. I couldn've go' drunk t'night. I wasn' in the mood.'

'Please! You must know how I feel.'

The bus stopped with a long skid.

'Barnetby crossroads!'

The blue light was switched on to allow the Waafs and their escorts to climb to the road. Somewhere among the tangle of bodies a voice shouted hoarsely, 'Lemme out! I gotta get out or I'll bust!'

'Me too! I'm nearly wetting my goddam pants!'

A dozen men stumbled to the roadside. Keith found his way to my side and breathed the outside air deeply. The men scrambled aboard and began stamping on the floor.

'Take it away!'

We started along the road that already was becoming familiar; the road between the beet fields, the haystacks and the roadside trees; the road between the squadron and the outer world. Outside our hut the bus dropped us. It carried its singing remnant up the road.

'Lagos Lagoon! Lagos Lagoon!
Belting black velvet in Lagos Lagoon!'

Someone was helping 'Bull' to our hut door.

'——didn' have a naughty. Jus' got drunk.'

The door shut behind them, leaving me standing with Keith in the darkness. We stood for some time without a word being spoken. The sky was completely clear, the stars shining with frigid brilliance.

By morning, ops were on again. Spirits among the crews were high, as the target was rumoured to be Turin. Italian targets were not considered worthy of a bomb painted on the aircraft's nose, being represented instead by ice-cream cones.

Geoff buttonholed me in the mess. 'We've got ourselves an engineer and a mid-upper gunner. You must meet them. The engineer is Welsh or half Welsh — Doug Richards —

and the mid-upper gunner lives somewhere near the camp — a lad named Frank Holmes.'

I met them that afternoon. Doug was sparely built and fair, a man with a lean, intelligent face. His expression was permanently quizzical owing to the absence of part of an upper eyelid that he had lost in an accident. He had been in the RAF ground crew since the Battle of Britain. On the ground we were to learn to laugh at him as a suave philanderer and a line-shooter, but while we were flying we were to find him a completely different man. In the air the most tractable and efficient of men might often become irritable and even dull-witted. With Doug this was reversed. During the most trying times we were to experience, he spoke as though in a drawing room. His efficiency was even heightened and his good-fellowship increased.

The seventh and final addition to our crew was as much part of Lincolnshire as the wolds themselves. Frank Holmes had warm, shrewd eyes that narrowed to good-humoured slits when he smiled. His hair was fair and his country-bred body was strong. Unlike many RAF sergeants, he was solidly independent and democratic in his outlook. His hobby was poaching. He lived near Elsham and poached chiefly on the estate of the neighbouring Earl of Yarborough.

''is gamekeeper suspects me. 'E says t' me t'oother day, "I'll get you yet, Frank, see if I dawn't now." T' ole boogger!'

Poaching appealed to 'Shag' immediately. We were often to see the two gunners leaving the camp by a path behind the barracks, one of them making futile attempts to conceal a double-barrelled shotgun under his battle dress. More often than not they returned empty-handed and once or twice were empty-handed and drunk. On one of these occasions they even opened fire within the boundaries of the camp, their target being the chimney of our room.

'Loocky we wuz droonk, or we'd ha' blown it off!'

But sometimes they returned in triumph and the crew would sit to potted partridge prepared by Frank's 'moother'. In times past, Frank and 'Shag' would have been among

England's finest soldiers — or, in peace, among her deported felons.

On this day that our crew was completed, the day of operations to Turin, Geoff, Max Burcher and I moved to a room opposite our original hut.

'The sooner the rest of the crew are together in rooms the better I'll be pleased. Barracks can be bad for morale.'

Remembering Porter and Hardisty and the others who had vanished from among us, I realized that Geoff was right. Porter's and Hardisty's beds were occupied now by strangers whose names we did not know and never were to know.

While I prepared to move to our new room, 'Bull' stood at his bedside putting on his ops clothing. When he had buttoned his battle dress over his white ops sweater, he came to me seriously.

'Listen, son, you're not going tonight. If anything happens to me, could you get my personal belongings home to my mother?'

I looked with astonishment at his ruddy face, taken unawares by the sudden change in him.

'I suppose the Air Force would do it, but you know the way it is.'

I stammered, 'They say the target's easy—'

'I know all about that, son, but I've got an idea. Anyway, you'd do that for me?'

'Of course.'

But that Turin could claim 'Bull' I refused to believe.

We slept that night in our new room and forgetfully left the curtains drawn. When I woke I realized that it was late. I flung back the curtains, releasing a stream of sunlight over Max and Geoff. Outside the day was fine. Before the hut opposite, the hut that had been ours, stood an empty van. I dressed hurriedly and crossed the road. Beside 'Bull's' bed stood the men of the Committee of Adjustment. I paused in the doorway, the realization striking me that I had let 'Bull' down. One of the men looked at me curiously, as though guessing my reason for being there. I turned away, wishing that I had risen earlier and that I had believed 'Bull' the night before.

We had only been three days on the squadron and had already seen over twenty men vanish from among our comparatively small numbers. Although worse days were to come, I remember this as my own most difficult period. In the North Sea gloom of that 1942 winter, I felt it would be impossible to wear the mask of indifference.

On the day that 'Bull' was lost, a Wellington from a neighbouring station approached Elsham Wolds to land. Suddenly it plunged from sight behind the hangars and with a frightful roar struck the ground. As the alarms sounded, I realized that I must not think; I must not visualize what had just happened; I must wear the impassive mask. Near the crew room I met Geoff.

'I just saw the prang,' he said.

I tried to speak casually. 'Anyone get out?'

'One. A farmer pulled out the rear gunner.'

After dinner, when most of the crews had left for Scunthorpe, F/O Henderson, the junior medical officer, came into the sergeants' mess. He asked me if I could go with him to the sick quarters to talk to the gunner from the crashed Wellington.

'He wants to see someone from Australia — I think a yarn might help him.'

The rear gunner appeared unscathed. He was in a dimly-lighted room, lying slightly propped up in bed. I recognized him as 'Brownie', a rowdy youngster with ginger hair, whose boots had been tried for size by his various friends the night before the flap to Bremen. Since those last days at Lichfield I had not seen him, nor did he appear to recognize me.

He addressed me as I came into the room.

'What part of Aussie are you from?'

'Victoria,' I said.

He appeared disappointed.

'Come from Perth m'self; good spot, too. Wouldn't mind being back there now, neither. Gee, it was a shaky do. I couldn' get away from the fire. Then this farmer bloke came — had an axe or something. He dragged me clear. Then I must have passed out.'

He paused, breathing heavily.

'Can't make out how it happened. Just seemed to go into a vertical dive. I called over the intercom, but couldn't get an answer. Then the great bloody flames——'

He lay back on his pillows, his eyes dilated. I wondered what to say to him, but in a moment he began talking again, rapidly and sometimes almost incoherently.

'That's my third prang. Overshot at Lichfield an' crashed into the canal. Then we hit a hill up north, an' now this. All dead. Can't make out how it happened. Nose first an' then the flames——'

'D'you reckon they'll make me fly again?' he asked suddenly.

He looked at me with alarmed eyes, but before I could answer him he said, 'I should; yes, I know I should fly again. But it shakes a bloke after three prangs. This was the worst, too. Guess I'll be over it in a few days an' then I'll fly again. But, gee, I don' want to think about it jus' now.'

'They'd only send you back if you were fit,' I said.

He made so much of this that I wished I had not said it.

'I might even get back home! Perth'd be all right, too. You don't know the West? Never get these freezin' days there.'

'My skipper is from Perth.'

'What's his name?'

'Geoff Maddern.'

'Old Maddern! That's right; knew him at Lichfield. Remember you now, too. You went on the Bremen flap. Nearly all them pilots was from the West — Syd Cook, Ted Laing, Col Bayliss — wonder where they are now?'

'Those three are here, at 103. They've gone out tonight. Tomorrow I'll tell them you're here.'

'Gee, I'd like to see them. Perhaps in the morning. I don't know what they're going t'do with me here. I feel OK

— I mean, nothin' broken. It's jus' those damn' flames. I go t' sleep an' keep dreamin' I'm back in the turret an' can't get away.'

He stopped for a moment and I noticed that his breathing had become easier.

'If they send me home — But I should fly more. Perhaps I could at home, though. Back roun' Perth. None o' these freezin' days —'

Before he had said more he was asleep. F/O Henderson appeared in the doorway.

'Good. We'll let him sleep.'

A few days after Brownie's crash Geoff came to us preening himself exaggeratedly.

'Right! You may now all buy me a drink. Just the big four-engine type — finished my circuits and bumps last night.'

'What do you think of the Hallies?'

He was unexpectedly non-committal.

'Not bad; not bad. By the way, we fly as a crew this afternoon.'

We climbed on a height test to 17,000ft, circling a part of England I shall always regard as ours. It was bounded to the north by the Humber and to the west by the silver line of the Trent. To the south it stretched as far as the pale cruciform of Lincoln Cathedral and to the east — that awesome direction — to the North Sea. Though the Halifax appeared to respond well to Geoff's handling, I remembered Doug's words on the ground before we took off: 'They're poor rudders on these kites. The bloomin' things even *look* a bad shape.' The story had already reached us that the Halifax Mark I had a vicious rudder stall and that few of those who experienced it came out alive.

But within two weeks our conversion to Halifaxes was almost over. Already two navigators of the conversion flight were to act as replacements on an operation to Cologne. One was to be Harry Wright, the other, a pilot officer named Munns. I knew Munns only slightly. He was older than most of us, with streaks of grey in his crinkled hair. I remembered that when we had discussed decorations one day, he had remarked, 'I'm not interested in gongs. My only wish is to get the business over and return to my wife and kiddy.' I saw then that he hated ops life, much as Keith Webber hated it. But he carried that additional and greatest of responsibilities — he was married and a father.

Our own crew had one exercise to do before going on to operations, a five-hour cross-country flight preceded by searchlight co-operation over Hull.

'Maddern, you will carry two army officers from Hull ack ack. They wish to observe the accuracy of their searchlights.'

We reached Hull a few minutes after take-off and plunged into searchlights. Geoff flew viciously, dodging and writhing in his efforts to throw off the beams. The airspeed needle was quivering at 310, and one of the officers was being unobtrusively sick on the floor, when we found ourselves at the centre of a German attack on Hull. The balloons were let up; the ack ack opened fire and a number of JU88s appeared in the searchlights. Our nose came up violently as Geoff attempted to top the balloons.

'Doug, fire the colours of the day!'

I saw Max Burcher double up with laughter.

'Wouldn't it slay you! Caught in their own flak!'

He went off into gales of laughter as we began our dive across the Humber with shells bursting close behind us.

'Navigator, we'll have to land at Elsham for more colours of the day before we do the cross-country.'

This seemed to suit the officers very well. The sick lieutenant managed a wan smile.

'We live to drink again!'

By the time we had returned from the cross-country flight the ops men had long been in. Harry Wright, we learned, was safe, but one other crew was missing. Not until morning did we hear that the crew was Winchester's. With his ops cap battered full of character and his long experience etched on his face, Winchester was almost the idealized RAF type. His navigator was Munns.

I walked to the mess under a weight of frustration that arose from my inability to answer the questions that crowded into my mind. Who had had the right to say to Munns, 'You must now kill the enemies of your country and prepare to have your life taken?' In ten years, would the loss of his life appear justifiable, or would it be evident that he had been led into a wrong or unnecessary course, that he had cast the pearl of his life before swine? Perhaps the only man who should go to Bomber Command was the man who had seen for himself that mass killing was the only way to a better world.

I knew, that day, that I had no such conviction. I felt in need of it. I wished that I could believe that we were bombing evil and making way for good. I wished that I could feel this with the intensity that a father would feel defending his family with no thought of himself. The only alternative was not to think. We had committed ourselves and could now do nothing. If our service life conflicted with our thinking, then our thinking must cease. We could not afford to fritter our strength on endless questioning, or in the luxury of frustration or sorrow. But on this day of Munns' death, as I walked to the mess, it was beyond my strength to stop thinking of the night's happenings.

Near the sports ground I looked up and saw a Waaf coming the other way. As we drew nearer I recognized Joan Sutherland. I decided suddenly that I would stop her. I would say, 'Why do you think we are fighting? Why do you think Munns has died?' As she reached me I turned to her. In her eyes there was gentle enquiry, as though she was aware that I wished to speak to her. I opened my mouth, but found nothing to say. She smiled and walked on.

That same morning we left the training unit and reported to the squadron. This involved little more than going from one long, low building with a concrete floor to another similar building fifty yards away. Two large rooms here were set

aside for crews. In one, fifteen or twenty men crowded about
a cylindrical stove. A few of them were reading; some were
talking, but many simply sat and smoked in obvious
boredom. In the adjoining room men about to fly were
preparing maps and logs at a large table. The walls here
were almost covered with notices and diagrams, diagrams
of a Halifax ditching; of Halifax engines; of a crew
abandoning a Halifax. Notices told of bombing practices;
of dangerous flying areas, and — the notice most read and
often the last read — the crew list for the night's operations.
For this notice the men about the stove were waiting.
Thousands of men were waiting for it all over England, and
because they spent most of their lives waiting to 'dice' they
waited restlessly.

We queued outside the Orderly Room door, waiting to
be asked a single question by the corporal there. The question
was this, "Oo d'yer want informed?" When we had given
him the names of our next of kin, we were sent to the crew
room to await the arrival of the Wing Commander. After
half an hour he came. I did not see him until an indignant
voice behind me addressed the crews sharply.

'Don't you stand up when your CO enters the room?'

I turned and saw a man of perhaps twenty-seven or
twenty-eight, tall and with a high complexion, higher now
than usual with anger. His eyes were blue-grey, his hair
receding. He wore RAF battle dress on which were the
ribbons of the DSO and DFC.

'Tonight there will be no operations.'

The news appeared to annoy him slightly, but among
the men there was visible relaxing.

'Squadron Leader Fox will see the new crews in this
room. The rest of you will report here again at one o'clock.'

We were left then with two squadron leaders, of whom
Fox was evidently the senior. He was compactly built and
somehow panther-like. His step was soft and full of spring;
his eyes narrowed and gleaming, as though he were keyed
always to high pitch. On his head was a shapeless ops cap,

and over his battle dress pocket was the ribbon of the DFM. The ribbon commanded our immediate respect. DFMs were seldom given for nothing, nor did many sergeants become squadron leaders.

The second squadron leader was Kennard. Besides a DFC he wore two operational adornments — the usual ops cap and a wide moustache. His eyes were dark and staring, as though constant peering into darkness had left them so. He was, I believe, little more than a boy, and it was sometimes said on the squadron that he wore his moustache to disguise his youth.

Fox sat casually on the table. 'I would like to have a yarn with you chaps who have just come to the squadron. I see that most of you are from Australia and one or two from Canada. I know that ideas of — uh — discipline are not quite the same in the colonies—

Beside me Geoff was on his feet. 'Excuse me, sir, we come from the Dominions!'

Fox looked at him disconcertedly. 'I — Yes, I had forgotten. You chaps do prefer the term "Dominions", don't you.'

Kennard stared at Geoff with more than usual intensity, as though noting his face for future reference. But from the men there were murmurs of agreement.

'In any case,' Fox continued, in a hardening voice, 'discipline among the sergeants has become very lax, and unless there is a big improvement we shall be obliged to tighten up on privileges.'

A week later Fox addressed the full squadron, bringing unbelievably good news.

'You will be glad to hear that we are to convert shortly to Lancasters.'

His voice was drowned by an outburst of cheering and shouting.

'Next week we take delivery of the first aircraft and will begin a period of intensive training. We are the first squadron in One Group to convert and the CO is anxious that we do so as quickly as possible.'

Looking back, I can see Fox clearly as he outlined the training scheme. He was still the narrow-eyed, panther-footed squadron leader, but he was also an enthusiastic boy. That night there were operations to Milan, one of the last operations on Halifaxes. Squadron Leader Fox, DFM, failed to return. Many months later, when we were among the senior crews on the squadron, Fox's navigator, 'Dizzy' Spiller, returned to the station. There were only two crews left on the squadron then who knew him and who had heard Fox's announcement of the change to Lancasters. Spiller was a cherubic Warrant Officer, famed for his casualness and for the bare minimum of navigational instruments he carried on ops. As casually as he had operated he had walked out of Europe and eventually, on that night many months later, had returned to his old crew room. He glanced about then for someone he knew, but only one man recognized him.

'Why, "Dizzy"! Walked out, eh? Did Fox get away?'

'Dizzy' shook his head. 'Bombs were dropped on us. Only one other chap got out — "Lofty" Maddocks, but he's a POW.'

'Dizzy' was the third navigator to escape during our early weeks on the squadron, the others being Pipkin and Mellor. Pipkin's escape was an epic which we once heard at lectures from him on escape technique, but I remember best the return of Mellor. We were sitting one evening in the mess, six weeks after Mellor had gone missing, when, looking up, we saw him standing in the doorway. No one spoke a word. He had long been considered dead and for some time his name had only been mentioned in a regretful sort of way. This shade of him glanced about the old haunts and then addressed us in a plaintive voice.

'Has anyone seen my greatcoat? I left it hanging here the night we went missing.'

Three days after the loss of Fox we huddled about the cylindrical stove discussing the latest rumour. It was said that the Wing Commander was anxious to have new crews do an operation on Halifaxes before converting to Lancasters. This was something we had hoped to escape, but at 11.30 the rumour was confirmed. The crew list went up and on it was the name of Maddern.

On the blackboard in the lecture room Kennard was writing the day's schedule:

Navigator's briefing 1300.
Main briefing 1400.
Meal 1500.
Final briefing 1600.
Take off 1700.

Each of these times was based on one ultimate time — our time over the target. Every step Bomber Command made was reckoned back from that final step.

I watched Kennard as he turned away from the board, his dark eyes staring from beneath his ancient ops cap, his wide moustache disguising his boyish face, the whistle worn as he alone wore it, on a cord over his shoulder. I wondered how he felt about Fox. They had always been spoken of together — Fox and Kennard. Now there was just Kennard waiting for Fox's successor. I looked for his reaction in his eyes, but found their watchful depths impossible to read.

'Navigators, you may go to lunch immediately.' I noticed by his voice that he had assumed authority. 'I have told the messes to have it ready for you. You will report to the navigation centre at 1300.'

The navigation centre was nothing more than a barracks with fifteen or twenty tables in place of the usual beds. At its far end was a platform and, on the wall behind the platform, a map of Europe. I lay my bag of maps and instruments on a table beside Keith Webber's table. This table was to remain mine for the whole of our time on the squadron and from it I was to see the navigator from almost every other table go missing; from some tables three or four navigators, from others more.

We waited uneasily until a Flight Lieutenant appeared at the doorway carrying a roll of charts. I remembered this officer as Magor, the organist at station church parades, a man who gave the impression of having recently wakened from a pleasant sleep. I heard later that he was a sick man and thus it was unlikely that his health would allow him to do a second tour of operations. His speech was spare and drawled.

'Is everyone here?' He glanced about with the same sleepy expression. 'Very well then, here are your charts.'

We spread them on the tables, glancing first at their eastern extremities. It was evident that the target was a distant one, as the chart extended to longitude 15° East. There was an undertone of discussion among the senior navigators, but I could not catch their suppositions. Magor walked slowly to the map of Europe.

'Here is your route. Base to Mablethorpe.' He pushed in a coloured pin at Mablethorpe and began extending a length of red wool. 'Mablethorpe to Position A, here on the Danish coast between Sylt and Esjberg. Position A, to Position B, here between Rostock and Lubeck. And Position B to the target, which is Stettin.'

'Stettin!' 'Stettin!'

It was whispered by a dozen voices. Magor waited for the exclamations to subside, then began the route home. It was directly across Europe, entering England again at Mablethorpe.

We had begun ruling the long cross-water legs on our charts when a number of the pilots joined us. Geoff, who was among them, was more than usually irritable, by which I knew that something was perturbing him.

'Where to?'

'Stettin.'

I ran my finger along the route.

'Hell! I guessed from the petrol load that we must be going a long way. It's going to be a dirty night — they reckon a fog is coming in.'

'We mightn't go.'

'Oh, we'll go all right.'

He stumped out of the room.

'I'll keep you a seat at main briefing.'

I went over my work a second time and was left last in the room. About me were bare tables, all disturbingly eloquent of the men who has passed before us. I pulled down the thread of wool that marked our route and left the room.

In the centre of the Headquarters building there was a room without windows. It had seating accommodation for a hundred and forty or so men and was lighted by chill fluorescent tubes. This was the main briefing room, the room we came to as crews as soon as navigators' briefing was over. I can see it now as it was that day and on the many days to follow, even to visualizing individual faces in the bluish haze from cigarettes. Newitt, the tall, fair Canadian; Berry, a big, boyish Englishman with puzzled eyes; Johnnie Roper, a typical RAF man, moustached and precise; my own skipper and crew, six men who were to become almost as familiar to me as my own brothers.

Sitting there waiting, the tension of the room enveloped us. I noticed the taut jaw muscles of the man in front of me; the staring darkness of Kennard's eyes; Ted Laing, his chin in his hand, his eyes on the map of Europe above the platform.

The Wing Commander was on the platform, his eyes more than usually fretful.

'Are you ready, Met?'

The lights were switched out and the beam of the epidiascope became the only illumination. A hundred pallid faces turned to the screen. The murmur of conversation subsided. Meredith, the senior meteorologist, began the forecast.

'The chart for tonight shows a high pressure system centred over the Midlands. It is moving very slowly indeed and should be somewhere in our vicinity by the time you return. This means, of course, a strong possibility of fog along the east coast for your return; in fact, it might extend considerably to the west.'

'What part of England is likely to remain clear, sir?'

'The far west — Cornwall.'

'What would our diversion be if we couldn't get in here?'

'St Eval.'

Meredith finished. On the screen appeared an aerial photograph of Stettin. An intelligence officer pointed out the docks, the submarine pens, the most heavily defended areas, our aiming point.

I began wondering what it was like always to brief men, never to see the actualities; always to notice the change of faces and to know that the men who had not returned had been lost over places such as this city of Stettin now revealed before us.

I could see the stooped figure of Keith Webber and, beside him, Tony Willis, their engineer. The men further away were dark, almost motionless shapes. The smoke had thickened to a bluish dusk, pricked by the glow of cigarettes.

The briefing officer had finished. In his sleepy voice Magor called for the lights. The darkness had lent the room a picture-show atmosphere of unreality, but beneath the all-revealing fluorescents I felt a surge of fear.

'The Wing Commander will explain tonight's tactics to you.'

Tactics had been complicated by low cloud over Europe and by the probability of fog on return. We were to go out to sea at low level and were to begin climbing as we neared the coast between Lubeck and Rostock.

'You have nine hours' petrol and a flight of eight hours twenty minutes. That calls for careful conservation of fuel.'

'What if we're diverted to St Eval?'

The Group Captain stood up in his place in the front row of seats.

'If a diversion to St Eval appears certain, I shan't permit the squadron to take off.'

He was still standing when an officer came in and handed him a signal. He glanced at it.

'Take off has been put back six hours until 2300. That should give base a chance to clear before you return at 0720.'

He sat down again and the Wing Commander took his place.

'Your operational meal will be at the usual tea time. I don't know that we can promise you eggs and bacon before you go and after you return——'

'Let's have them before we go!' shouted someone. 'Let's be sure of them.'

'All right; before you go, then. After the meal, crews will have time to go to the first house at the pictures. Report to the crew room at 2130.'

In twos and threes we drifted towards the mess. Geoff was even more irritable then before.

'They've taxied the kites into line round the perimeter track and are topping up the tanks. It's a pretty poor show if we're to end up as short of petrol as that!'

'We mightn't go,' said Ted. 'The wind has dropped. If the fog comes it will probably stay.'

'That only means we'll be sent to St Eval. I wonder what they expect us to fly on?'

By the time we went to the pictures it was dusk. The evening was calm with the first bite of winter chilling our faces. As we walked to the camp cinema the sound of an engine being tested before the flight came to us clearly, a full-throated roar that brought back memories of our take-off for Bremen the night Joe Turnbull's crew had crashed at Lichfield.

In the cinema — which was also the church and the gymnasium — officers sat in the front row. Behind them sat the NCOs and, well to the rear, the 'other ranks'. Among the 'other ranks' I saw Joan Sutherland. She was alone and I thought she smiled slightly. I had dropped behind the crew when I heard a snort from Geoff, 'Come on, navigator — keep your eyes off the Waafs!'

In the darkness all thought of Stettin became unreal. After the show we would catch a tram home and there sit awhile drinking tea and discussing the film before a blazing fire. But the film, when it began, aggravated our tension. It was a tale of wrecks and treachery at sea. There were underwater shots of long-dead ships and of grotesque sea monsters — all this accompanied by restless music. Sometimes the music was interrupted by calls on the tannoy for an electrician, an armourer, or a mechanic. At such moments it was impossible to forget that outside the ground crew were preparing for our departure. Stettin! Stettin! The name repeated itself like hammer blows on the mind.

On the screen a man was battling on a schooner through a storm at sea as shortly we would battle eastward. The men about me were silent, each one knowing nothing of the mind of the man beside him. Stettin! Unexpectedly the sound of the storm faded. An amplified voice boomed through the theatre.

'All night flying has been cancelled! Repeat: All night flying has been cancelled!'

The storm was drowned by spontaneous cheering. We settled back in our seats to enjoy the film. Twenty-four hours of security; twenty-four wonderful hours!

CHAPTER FIVE

Lancasters

Next morning we prepared again for Stettin, but with the knowledge that this would be the swansong of the Halifaxes. When we went to main briefing the day was again clear and calm. To our consternation we found that Frank and 'Shag' were missing from their places. Geoff glanced about for them anxiously.

'I'll break their damn' necks. I know what they're doing — I saw Frank just after lunch with a bloody great gun under his arm.'

Somehow we covered up for them, but halfway through briefing they blundered in, their shadows blotting out the target picture on the screen.

'Sit down at the back!'

They stumbled past us, reeking of expended cartridges.

'Sorry, Geoff. It wuz the keeper — run us into a corner, just when we got a big cock pheasant an' all.'

'Silence, that man!'

We did not hear the rest of their story until long after. Perhaps they were afraid of police action, or of being hauled before the Earl himself. They had been cornered by the gamekeeper. With hedges on two sides of them, Frank had acted quickly. Pointing the gun at one of the hedges, he had fired both barrels, blowing a hole through which they had managed to claw their way.

As they panted their excuses that afternoon I began to feel better fitted to meet the business ahead — and I knew that half my strength had come from the crew's two poachers.

We were sitting down to our meal when the tannoy erupted cheerfully, 'All night flying is cancelled. Repeat: all night flying is cancelled.'

At this unexpected reprieve pandemonium broke out. There was one predominant shout — 'Goodbye, Halliebags!'

Lancasters, we found, were to be delivered next day.

In the morning the first of them circled Elsham. We watched them sweep down to our runway, clean-lined and lady-like, a contrast with the more robust, masculine lines of the Halifaxes. We saw them coming like relief coming to a hard-pressed army; they were unconquerable; the days of heavy losses were over. Soon there was a Lancaster at each dispersal point and no sign of the Halifaxes. Perhaps they were not sufficiently superior to Halifaxes to warrant our enthusiasm, but we would have been cheered by any change that held hope of lower losses.

One day, soon after the changeover, I sat in a swivel chair before the large, green navigator's table of B Beer waiting to set out on an eight-hour cross-country flight, the last exercise of our conversion. It was mid-afternoon, clear over Lincolnshire, but banked with cloud along the northern horizon. The fields and villages shrank below as we climbed to 6,000ft. We crossed the coast at Whitby and turned nor' nor' west for Kinnaird's Head. Within half an hour we were over cloud, white and unbroken for as far north as we could see. The fields and hedges had gone and gone the coast and the crawling steamers; we were England's no longer, but flew alone with the sun in an empty sky.

All the way to Kinnaird's Head I worked steadily at the chart, checking first on Gee, that mysterious radar aid then coming into general use, and then by radio bearings on northern stations. Once, for no more than a minute, I joined Geoff and Doug in the glass-enclosed cockpit. Cloud still lay below us, a deep-piled carpet beneath the dome of the sky. West beyond the Scottish Lowlands the sun was blazing its last, flushing the whole remote world. The crew was watching intently, staring northward.

I worked inside for twenty minutes more, then returned to the cockpit. Outside the scene had changed. The sun had gone, leaving the floor below us grey and very lonely. The sky above was empty of clouds and as yet of stars. Geoff peered more intently ahead, his eyes puckered. At his right knee the face of the compass glowed green, the needle oscillating on 338 degrees, the course I had given him. As I stood there the darkness thickened and the stars appeared, cold droplets of light in an empty world. The full realization settled on me that these other men were trusting me to guide them through this inhospitable sky, and that such would be my task until our operational life was over.

Our first operation from the squadron passed uneventfully. Somehow we reached Frankfurt and somehow we returned. Over the target one sentence from the Master Bomber reached us in a precise but troubled voice. 'You are bombing away to hell south—' Then the voice — and perhaps the speaker — was swallowed up in the onslaught.

On the long return journey bursts of horizontal tracer from nearby air-to-air battles frequently split the night, ending sometimes in mid-air explosions. But our own journey was uneventful, so uneventful that I was concerned that the crew might imagine ops navigation to be little different from the cross-country exercises to which we were so accustomed.

On our return, Lincolnshire lay beneath fog. We were diverted soon after dawn to Middleton-St-George, in County Durham, the home aerodrome of a Canadian bomber squadron. There we remained for two more days, grounded by fog. Although we borrowed collars and ties from the Canadians and spent those two days in the pubs and cinemas of Middlesborough, the realization was with me constantly that my ops navigation was haphazard and dangerous. It was obvious that to have any chance of surviving a tour we could not afford to meander across Europe with little real idea of our whereabouts.

On our return we were briefed for Mannheim. Again we meandered across Europe, found our target and bombed. But on the return journey the blow I had anticipated fell.

About an hour out from the target, an astro fix showed us 40 miles south of track. On training flights my star shots had brought good results, but I regarded this fix with extreme doubt. Astro on operations was a different proposition. With surprise attacks by fighters always a probability, none of us regarded straight and level flight with much enthusiasm, with the result I tended to work hurriedly and less accurately. To alter course on this one check appeared to be inviting trouble. To get another fix was soon complicated by the development of high cloud. Our Gee and our radio were both out of order, and, in any event, we were beyond the range of British transmitters. I continued with dead reckoning for almost two hours. For all that time a strong wind blew us further and further south of track. Supposedly at Caen, we turned for Dungeness, and supposedly at Dungeness, we turned for Elsham. We must in fact have been in the northern reaches of the Bay of Biscay. Below us there was still a layer of cloud; above, windblown cirrus.

I was waiting to hear Ted's reassuring announcement, 'I can see a beacon through a break in the cloud — probably somewhere on the south coast,' when there was a cry from the rear turret, 'Flak dead astern!'

I jumped to my feet. We should by this time have crossed the English coast.

'Flak coming straight up!'

We swung off course.

'Navigator, where the hell are we? When we get out of this muck, what about a bit of astro?'

I shuffled to the astro-dome, panting as though deprived of air. The dome was almost over the W.Op's head, being shielded from his light by a black curtain. The curtain was closely drawn, as beneath the light Max was trying to find the fault in his set.

'I need a star shot,' I said.

'How the hell am I going to work in the dark?'

'We must have a check.'

'Well, do you want this set fixed, or don't you?'

'Give me two minutes.'

Growling something, he switched off the light. I pulled back the curtain and raised my head into the glass bubble.

Sometimes those moments return to me. With sudden clarity I see Max Burcher trying to repair his set and feel the sextant again cold in my hands, and hear the voices of Geoff and Doug discussing our fuel. With that, the emotions of that night come flooding back: I am to blame for our predicament; I am flinging away the lives of a crew.

'Hello, Darkie; hello, Darkie; hello, Darkie! This is Hazel B beer calling; Hazel B beer. Are you receiving me? Are you receiving me? Are you receiving me? Over to you, over!'

Geoff's distress call was familiar from our training. I strained my ears, but there was no suggestion of a reply.

Max touched my leg. 'Haven't you finished yet?'

'One more shot.'

I looked outside again. There was now no light of any kind. Dimly I could see the aircrews thrusting us further into the unknown. The thought struck me that we could be heading north between England and the Continent with land falling away on either side. This sudden suspicion brought a moment of paralysis. I stood for perhaps ten seconds staring at the now unclouded array of stars, doing nothing. Geoff was finishing his call for the second time.

'Are you receiving me? Are you receiving me? Over to you, over!'

There was still no reply. The men were silent. I realized then that my chief fear of ops had been this fear, the fear of wasting the lives of other men. I cast about urgently for Spica to complete my fix. Again Geoff was calling. I listened closely but heard nothing. Then 'Shag', who was isolated from the engine noise, suddenly called us.

'There was an answer! Call again!'

The call was repeated. This time we heard a voice, but what it said we were unable to tell. Again 'Shag' had heard more clearly.

'It's in English, but I can't get it!'

Geoff called again. Clearly from below came the voice of a girl.

'Hello Hazel B beer! Hello Hazel B beer! This is Thorney

Island replying; Thorney Island replying.'

Ahead through breaking cloud we saw the searchlights of Portsmouth. Somehow we reached Waddington, our six hours' petrol stretched to seven hours forty-five minutes.

We flew to Elsham next morning, our mood unusually subdued. By the time we had landed it was too late for the aircraft to be prepared for the night's operation, but, early next morning, Doug came to our room.

'We're to operate tonight in L London.'

'Damn' them!' Geoff sat up irritably in bed. 'We were in L that night with the army wallahs over Hull. Everyone says that it's only lucky for Roly Newitt. It brings every other crew trouble.'

Doug stood by consolingly. 'Should be an easy trip, though — a gardening stooge. We make a landfall, do a timed run and sow the mines.'

Geoff brightened slightly. 'Where to?'

'Not a clue — except that a fair load of petrol is going on.'

We went to the crew room lightheartedly. Mining, everyone said, was easy. By mid-afternoon my optimism had diminished. Our route led deep into the islands of the Baltic, the first leg jumping from Mablethorpe some 400 miles to Kobing Fiord. The night promised to be cloudy, the cloud increasing as we neared the target.

'You are to cross the North Sea at two thousand feet, then drop to one thousand feet or lower over Denmark. Only six aircraft will be taking part, as Bomber Command's main attack tonight will be in the Lorient-St Nazaire area.'

The briefing officer handed us white Admiralty charts.

'Here are your plots. Cook, you will sow your vegetables in this plot; Maddern, in this ——'

We looked closely at a section of Copenhagen Sound, trying to imprint it on our memories.

Take-off was extremely early. By mid-afternoon we were sitting in L London waiting to leave. By five o'clock we were in sight of neither land nor the few other aircraft. The evening was calm and grey, the horizon limited by low-hanging wisps of cloud. Below us the North Sea stirred sluggishly, unmarked by whitecaps. As the Gee was directed south to aid the main attack, we reached the limit of its special chart at only 3° east. With little else to do, I continued to copy down the instrument readings, although no longer able to plot them. For this I was later thankful.

The sea crossing passed uneventfully. At 1845 Ted sighted Kobing Fiord. The twilight was fading rapidly, but the flat coastland of Denmark lay clearly on the face of the sea. In the north the aurora borealis had begun its ceaseless undulating movements, like a heavenly curtain blown by the wind.

We checked several details of the topography until no doubt existed in my mind that this was Kobing Fiord. We began to lose height, first to 1,000ft, then almost to ground level. The cloud base, which had been 3,000ft over the sea, was lowering considerably. Over northern Denmark the night was quiet. Cars with headlights scarcely dimmed sped between white, box-like cottages. We flew over hamlets and skirted towns, flying so low that, but for our engines, we could have spoken to people in the streets. Our nearness to them accentuated the feeling of fantasy that often came to me, the feeling of being so near yet so very far from the hidden life of Europe.

At the east coast we plunged into cloud. The main base had fallen to 500ft, with lower patches. Clouds took the appearance of islands and islands of clouds. We began searching anxiously for our pinpoint, but could at first see no sign of it. At the flare shute Max Burcher was becoming impatient.

'Look, if you can't see, let me drop a flare.'

'And 'ave night fighters jump us!'

'Well, if we hang about here long enough it's just as bad.'

'I see it now,' said Ted, 'there, straight ahead. If you can time your run from that point, Geoff.'

We turned towards it into increasing cloud and drizzling rain.

'Over the point now — you can start counting, navigator.'

I began counting ten-second intervals.

'Speed it up!'

'— nine, ten, drop!'

There was no flak and not a single searchlight, but something eerie about the place gripped us. Somewhere not far below, the sea was accepting our mines, cradling them till their hour came. The task was soon over. We turned back for Kobing Fiord, a distance of 150 miles. The night was even quieter than before. We saw no houses, no roads and no cars. At 1,000ft occasional patches of cloud still blotted out our vision.

'We should be over the sea soon, shouldn't we?'

'Three minutes to go,' I said.

At the end of three minutes Geoff said quietly, 'We're still over land. What do you want me to do?'

As the coast must obviously have been near at hand I answered, 'Keep on this course for five more minutes.'

Five minutes meant nearly 20 miles, which I knew would put us safely out to sea. Geoff flew in silence. The minutes slipped by rapidly, but at the end of them he said, 'We are still over land and there are searchlights ahead!'

The situation became suddenly fantastic. Our distance to run was 150 miles, yet Geoff, though steering north-west, was taking more than an hour to reach the sea. Either we were not over Denmark at all, or we were not steering north-west as the compass undeniably showed. The memory of our last strange operation was so clear in my mind that I was inclined to the more extreme idea. I turned to Max.

'See if England is within range. I don't suppose you'll get much, but it might be a check.'

He nodded and began rotating the loop.

'Searchlights! A bunch of them to starboard.'

I felt Geoff swing away, losing height. Searchlights sprang up nearer us, again to starboard, pushing us to port.

I looked at my chart. We had set course truly enough from Kobing Fiord to our mining place and truly enough back again. If we had flown north-west from the Baltic, Denmark would have been long behind us. But if we had flown south-west? I found myself repeated it. 'If we have flown south-west. If we are somehow tracking diagonally across Denmark towards Esjberg, or Sylt—'

I spoke to Geoff again. 'Turn starboard ninety degrees —'

'Don't be damned silly! We're in flak.'

As he spoke the first near miss burst below us. I stood gripping the table and listening. A cannonade like a roll of drums swept our full length, followed by a single, distinct explosion that tilted us sharply.

'Hit our wing! Doug, I'm lowering my seat — I can't see for searchlights.'

The searchlights swung horizontally along the ground, lighting us clearly. Geoff pulled over them, but they swung upward, forcing him to drop low.

'You're nearly into trees!'

A constant spray of light flak was being directed at us from ahead and to port, each flash of the guns lighting up the gunners in the pits. Frank and 'Shag' concentrated on one as we passed. They fired until the whole position vanished in smoke and flame. Max still sat at his set, looking slightly annoyed at the interruption to his work. He had risen from his seat when the flak closed on us. It snapped and roared at our flanks and belly, each shot louder than the last, till a sudden yellow flash threw me against the fuselage. As I fell, I listened for the shot that must finish us. But the shell bursts had ceased. I felt then for my intercom switch.

'Everyone OK?'

The line was dead. Faintly above the roar of the engines I heard my name called. Turning, I saw Max, looked at me out of a torn face. He was holding his right arm from his side, regarding it with a bewildered, almost childlike expression, then looking back at me. The arm had been badly hit by shrapnel, so that the muscle protruded in several places. On the floor at his feet his shell dressing was burning. I stamped it out and took down another.

'How's my face?' he asked suddenly.

'Congealing already.'

'My nose?'

'Just missed it.'

'I thought it had gone!' He smiled wryly, managing to look diabolical.

I bandaged his arm and began looking for other wounds. A crooked gash ran from his eye to his nose, but was almost completely congealed. A third piece of shrapnel had skipped the base of his throat; a fourth had gouged his chest; a fifth had hit the back of his hand. What had missed him had gone out through the astro-dome. With his arm bandaged, he crawled over the mainspar to the rest position and settled there under two Irvin jackets.

'How do you feel?'

'Fine.'

He grinned diabolically again. 'Lucky I wasn't standing in the astro-dome as I usually am — would have got the lot in the head.'

I noticed clearly for the first time that we were flying more or less straight and level and that the firing had ceased. The sound of the engines was strong and unbroken. Beside Max's position there was a rent in the fuselage. His set appeared, at a glance, to have been smashed irreparably, while my own belongings lay on the floor in a welter of blood, ashes and spilt coffee. I tore a corner off the chart and scribbled on it, 'Max hit. Steer 280° magnetic.' I reached through beside the blackout curtain to Doug. He took the note and a moment later his head appeared in our compartment.

'On course. How's Max?'

'OK, I think.'

'It was their last shot — we were right on the coast.'

I went down the fuselage to the gunners. Neither of them

had been hit, nor did there appear to be any further damage to the aircraft. As I passed Max he asked how we were going.

'Well on the way home,' I said.

'How far now?'

'Not much over three hundred miles.'

In the debris on the floor I found the paper on which were scribbled the unplottable Gee readings taken on the outward journey. By comparing them with the readings I was able to get now, I could follow the track we had flown going out. Beside each of the outbound readings was the time at which it had been taken, which meant that I was able to estimate our homebound speed.

Several times during the return journey, Max crawled over the mainspar and attempted to repair his set, but as we neared the Humber I saw him bite his lip in pain. We left the shadowy mouth of the river on our right. The R/T being useless, we fired distress signals over Elsham, till a green light flashed from the edge of the aerodrome. We let down through the darkness, lined up and landed. Racing level with us was an ambulance.

I went down the fuselage to the rear door and opened it, letting in the fresh air. As we pulled up, three figures jumped from the ambulance. The first two were the MOs, Gauvain and Henderson.

'Anyone hurt?'

'Burcher, sir.'

When they had passed me, I noticed the third figure. It was the Wingco. He climbed into the aircraft, and as he did so I heard him mutter in a strangely distressed voice,

'These damned mine-laying trips!'

I suddenly warmed to him, seeing a different man from the man he had to be as Wing Commander.

'Bad luck, Maddern! Hurry out and get some tea.' He turned to Max, whose face was now grey through the blood. 'How do you feel, Burcher?'

'Fine, thanks, sir.'

Gauvain leaned towards me. 'Did you give him morphine?'

I shook my head. 'He was quite bright until just before we landed.'

'That's all right. He's a tough man.'

Geoff cut the motors, casting us into silence. The doctors and the Wingco helped Max to the ambulance. For the first time since we had left Denmark we heard Geoff's voice clearly, and what he said I have always remembered.

'I never want to fly with another crew. This one will do me.'

In the morning the full significance of our shaky do struck me. Twice in succession I had failed the crew. Now Max lay in hospital and an incoherent, blood-stained log of mine was on Magor's table. The whole business weighed heavily on my mind, seeming at first a monstrous impossibility, then an only too real calamity. We went to see Max directly after parade. He began to smile, but winced.

'Don't make me smile — it hurts!'

Doc Henderson was examining his face. 'We'll have those stitches out in a few days and you'll hardly see a mark.'

'It's likely to keep you off flying for a while. When it's better we'll have to see if you can manipulate your morse key properly.'

Max looked despondent. 'Do you think I'll lose my crew?'

Doc Henderson evaded the subject cheerfully. 'It's too early to say yet — I think you have a good chance of catching up with them.'

But the fact was that Max had lost a third of the muscle of his right arm and stood no chance of rejoining us at all.

I walked down the road with Geoff, making up my mind that in a moment I would say to him, 'After the last couple of trips, I think it would be best for the crew if I pulled out.' Probably he would say, 'Don't be damned silly — every crew has a few tough trips.' But, in all fairness, I should point out that on both occasions I was uncertain of our whereabouts. During our training, luck had been with me, but to survive operations a navigator needed luck and skill as well. Without either, a crew was doomed.

'We're supposed to go to a bull talk at eleven,' mumbled Geoff over a cigarette, 'This place is like a damned kindergarten.'

'Who wants us this time?'

'The Wingco again — don't know what about.'

The talk concerned causes underlying our recent losses. Night fighters, it was believed, were causing over seventy per cent of them. The next biggest cause was navigational errors.

'Too many aircraft are wandering off track and finding themselves caught over defended towns.'

I held my breath, staring at the Wing Commander over the hundred heads of the squadron.

'Because of navigational inaccuracies, Maddern's crew ran into trouble on the last operation.'

The hundred heads and the face of the Wing Commander receded. I dared not look at the men of my crew. I only knew that I must let them have a new navigator. What followed I have forgotten. I went later to our room and when Geoff came in I spoke.

'After that the crew deserves a new navigator,' I said.

Geoff was stooping over the stove. He stood up and exclaimed as I had imagined him exclaiming, 'Don't be damned silly!'

After the brief exchange that followed, I decided to go with the crew once more.

Life on the squadron was seldom far from fantasy. We might, at eight, be in a chair beside a fire, but at ten, in an empty world above a floor of cloud. Or at eight, walking in Barnetby with a girl whose nearness denied all possibility of sudden death at twelve.

Two days after our incident over Denmark I felt this contrast strongly. Unexpectedly we had been granted two days' leave while a replacement was being found for Max Burcher. I went to Surrey and, on the second morning, walked from Horley down the Brighton Road to Povey Cross. I found myself there in a lane so heavily shaded that frost still lay on the roadside grass, though it was after ten o'clock. I had turned into it with one thought driving all others from my mind: that this lane led to the village of Charlwood and that it was from Charlwood I believed my family to have come.

Until 1850 my great-grandfather and his sons had been booksellers and printers in Norwich. In that year they had transferred their business to Melbourne and there they had settled. This was as much as we knew with certainty, but it was sometimes vaguely remarked that the family had come originally from a village in Surrey which was said to bear our name.

Charlwood was not marked on either of the RAF maps issued us, but when we transferred to the squadron I found a military survey in the crew room. Charlwood appeared on it as a cluster of buildings three miles from Horley.

The Charlwood lane brought me at length to an avenue of trees. Ahead there was a cricket field and near it a few cottages. Disappointed that there was so little to see, I walked in a different direction. I had not gone far when I saw a church tower rising above trees. In the east face of it a clock showed twenty past eleven. I noticed then a winding path that appeared to lead to the church. I turned into it, walking on flat, irregular stones, called locally 'causies'. The path was hemmed closely by elms, the leaves from which had covered the causies deeply. A hedge linked elm to elm, following each turn of the path until after perhaps 200 yards, the path ended, leaving me in a short street.

I stood between a grey church and a green-and-white inn. The inn carried a board with the name and sign of the 'Half Moon'. I saw, too, a post office and one or two shops, all concealed within the short street. Neither in the street nor about the church was there a soul to be seen, though somewhere further away ducks were quacking and someone was hammering. The church, I saw, had two naves, lying parallel, evidently of different periods.

I was about to go into it when I noticed a number of Remembrance Day wreaths at the foot of the war memorial nearby. On one was the name, Charlwood W.I., the initials following the name as was done in the Services. I was looking at it when a woman appeared, carrying a shopping basket. I asked her if W.I.Charlwood lived in the village. She appeared puzzled, so I pointed to the wreath.

She smiled. 'Oh, Charlwood W.I. — that wreath was from the Women's Institute.'

I felt disappointed and foolish. 'Is there no one by the name of Charlwood living here, then?'

'No,' she answered, looking at me curiously.

'It happens to be my name,' I said.

She suddenly comprehended. 'Your people came from here?'

'I believe so.'

Her eyes widened. 'You must meet the Rector! I'm on my way to the shops, but if you can wait I shall introduce you.'

Having arranged to meet at twelve, we parted.

I followed a path through the lychgate to the porch. Its arched entrance had been fretted by the rain and wind of centuries and worn by the hands of countless people. I passed through into the church, away from the few sounds of the village. Standing inside the door, I realized that my family had lived in Australia for only ninety years. It was probable that before those years they had come here to their baptisms, their devotions and their marriages, and probably had been borne to nearby graves.

I remained there till the clock in the tower chimed twelve, releasing its slow waves of sound through the empty church. Going outside, I saw that the woman I had met was coming up the path from the village, her basket filled. She led me round the west end of the church and through a hedged walk to the rectory. About the house spread smooth lawns. Trees rose beside the drive and ducks sailed on the glebe pond.

The rector was a spare Ulsterman, his face strong and his eyes fearless. His wife was of Scottish extraction: animated, interested and youthful in manner. As they were about to sit down to lunch they asked me to join them.

I remember that during the meal there was often silence. Sometimes we spoke briefly of the reasons that had brought me to the village, but for much of the time there was a constraint over us that I found in the first moments of many another English meeting. The war was not mentioned. Sitting there, looking out on to the lawns and the church, I began to feel that these two people could know little of its anxiety and danger. Once this thought had entered my mind, it enlarged itself until I began to speak of squadron life and the men I had known.

At that the rector and his wife appeared almost apologetic for the peace surrounding them. Bomber Command losses, they knew, were terrible and England deeply appreciated the men who had come from the other side of the world.

Soon after this the meal ended and we went to the study fireside. Sitting before the blaze of logs with the trees of Charlwood nodding against the sky outside, I saw on the mantelpiece the photographs of three young men. With a good deal of embarrassment I asked if they were the rector's sons.

They were, but they had not been home for a long time. Bob had been taken prisoner in Hong Kong, but had escaped across China and was now with Wingate in Burma. Pat, a major at twenty-two, had been taken prisoner in Singapore. It was over a year since they had had news of him. Jim was in North Africa.

Hong Kong; Singapore; North Africa.

For a long time none of us spoke, but the longer the silence lasted the more I realized that I must speak. I exclaimed at last, 'When I came here I thought how peaceful your home was and how far from the atmosphere of the squadron. I didn't imagine that you had such anxieties.'

The two were looking at me. I realized that this un-

English outbreak might well repel them. I concluded lamely, 'I shall never jump to conclusions in England again.'

To my relief the barrier of constraint fell away. We relaxed by the fire, as I was to relax there often in the days ahead. We had been sitting there for some time when an incident occurred that guided the remainder of my Charlwood search. A neighbour of the rector's came excitedly to the door. He had found, he said, the grave of a James Charlwood, who had been born in the reign of George III and had died five years after Waterloo.

We left the room and hurried across the lawn. Perhaps ten feet from the west end of the church he showed us two plain grey stones, covered with years of lichen. Stooping before the nearer, we read the name JAMES CHARLWOOD and the year of his death, 1820.

I knew, then, that this was indeed our village and that close by lay the remains of my great-great-grandfather, whose son had gone to Australia in 1850.

By scraping the stone we uncovered the full inscription:

IN
MEMORY OF
JAMES CHARLWOOD
WHO DIED FEBRUARY 4th 1820
AGED 48 YEARS
AS HE DEPARTED TRUSTING ON THE BLESSED REDEEMER
WE HUMBLY HOPE THAT HE WILL BE FOUND WITH THE
MILLIONS OF BLOOD — BOUGHT SOULS OF WHOM IT IS
SAID,
FOR THE LAMB WHICH IS IN THE MIDST OF THEM SHALL
FEED THEM AND LEAD THEM UNTO LIVING FOUNTAINS OF
WATER AND GOD SHALL WIPE AWAY ALL TEARS FROM
THEIR EYES

On the stone nearby only three letters remained uncovered, but by scraping away the lichen we revealed its full inscription. It marked the grave of Phoebe, wife of James, who had died in 1816.

The words from Revelation were continued:

GOD SHALL WIPE AWAY ALL TEARS FROM THEIR EYES AND
THERE SHALL BE NO MORE DEATH NEITHER SORROW NOR
CRYING NEITHER SHALL THERE BE ANY MORE PAIN, FOR
THE FORMER THINGS ARE PASSED AWAY

It was by now mid-afternoon. With the rector and his wife I went to the vestry to search the registers for the name of James Charlwood. We found it with little difficulty, then searched progressively older registers, till in faded and cramped writing we found Thomas, born in 1682. Beyond his name we were unable to go. I knew of John Charlwood, the Elizabethan printer, but whether he too had come from Charlwood village I could not learn. Not until 1951, when two Surrey women published a book on Charlwood, did we learn of a reeve of the village in the thirteenth century. His name was De Cherlewode.

By the time our search had ended it was late afternoon. That night I had to return to Elsham and to all that the name implied. Before we left the church I climbed the narrow stairs to the tower, passing on the way six bells, immobile and slumbering. In the dim light I read on one the words, 'William Eldridge made me 1668' and on another, 'William Eldredge made mee 1662'.

I stepped out into the chill air. Below lay the village, much as it had been known to the Charlwoods whose names I had found in the register: the 'Half Moon'; the few shops; the Street, as it was called; the cottages, half hidden among their trees; the home of Wickens, the builder, whose family name appeared in the records for as far into the past as they reached; the swelling turf of the churchyard with its whitened stones ...

I reached London by dusk and King's Cross soon after. At Elsham the Lancasters were missing from their places. The flarepath was alight, awaiting their return.

Next morning the aircraft were loaded with mines. With the exception of one crew, the squadron was to mine the mouth of the river Garonne, but within half an hour of take-off Command had not finalized the route. The one crew,

Smith's crew, was to mine somewhere in Danish waters. While the navigators worked frantically at each change of route, the rest of the crew lay ready dressed about the room. They were surrounded by the usual paraphernalia of bomber men: Irvin jackets; coffee flasks; pigeons in metal containers; helmets and oxygen masks. Some stared moodily from the windows; others lay waiting with eyes closed, their heads pillowed on their parachutes. Outside a fog was thickening rapidly, transforming familiar objects into things grotesque and obscure.

My work was not half complete when the NCO in charge of transport began calling us to the buses. At this moment the Wing Commander hurried from his office.

'The Garonne trip is scrubbed! P/O Smith is still to do the other job. The rest of you may go.'

The men sprang to their feet. Kennard came in, rubbing his hands. 'A special bus for Scunthorpe in half an hour!'

As I groped with Geoff through the fog, we planned to visit Max Burcher. It was rumoured that he was to be moved to an Air Force hospital. We opened our door and lit the fire.

'Too close to be nice,' I said.

Geoff grunted concurringly. 'I can't see why they must send one kite. I'm damned glad it isn't us.' He walked to the window while he put his collar on. 'Just look at the fog! I don't think they'll let Smithy go.'

We stepped outside and began walking to the Sick Quarters. There was no sound other than the drip of water from indistinct trees, but we strained our ears for something else. We had not gone far when we heard it — a 'plane starting up on the far side of the aerodrome. We stood listening while the fog misted our coats. As it began taxiing we stared in the direction of the sound. I imagined Smithy staring as we were into the vaporous wall, and Hewitt, his navigator, stooped over his chart, a sharp ache at the pit of his stomach. We were near the Sick Quarters when the Lancaster began gathering speed, coming fast towards us. For no more than a second we saw the vague bulk of it pass through the mist overhead. Gradually its roar came to us more quietly, a sound dreadfully lonely and pregnant with fear. It had scarcely died when we heard the Scunthorpe bus and its singing passengers. It passed us in the fog, the men bellowing the usual songs.

What happened to P/O Smith we never knew. By the time the Scunthorpe bus had returned, his crew had met their end. The North Sea, or those coasts of Denmark we remembered so well, were the possessors of his secret.

We found Max sitting on the edge of his bed. The stitches had been removed from his face, but it was evident that the mending of his arm would be a long business. Next day he was to be sent to the RAF base hospital at Rawceby, so it was apparent that he could not hope to catch up with us. We did not discuss the matter, but left him as though expecting him in the crew again within a few weeks.

Courageous Max. His morse arm was damaged more than he knew, but by persevering he fitted himself once more for ops. As he was far too late to rejoin us, he was sent to 460 Squadron, an all-Australian squadron in Lincolnshire. Soon after this posting he was killed on an operation to Hamburg. We were to see many a pilot and many an officer decorated for showing spirit no greater than Max had shown. But for every five DFC's the Air Force awarded, it awarded only one DFM, and few of these indeed went to mere wireless operator-air gunners.

We met Max's successor next day, an RAF flight sergeant who had already completed a tour over Europe. Graham Briggs was one of those very few non-pilot NCOs who wore the DFM. Had it not been for its finely striped ribbon we would have thought him sleepy, phlegmatic and indifferent.

In thinking him phlegmatic we might have been right. I was often to feel in our hours over Europe that Graham imagined himself riding in a London taxi to the dullest imaginable appointment. And sleepy he undoubtedly was. Often on operations I was to tap him with my long rule, thinking he had fallen asleep completely, but invariably he was to retort with a wide-awake air, 'I'm listenin' out to base!' But in imagining him to be indifferent we would have been completely wrong. What might have been mistaken for indifference in him was that streak of contemptuous serenity so often noticeable in the bearing and eyes of experienced ops men. In his eyes was the same strange staring I had seen in theirs.

He was a Leicestershire man and spoke with what we supposed must be a Leicestershire accent and idiom. When we met I said, 'I've just heard that you are coming into the crew.'

He stared at me disconcertingly for a very long time.

'Ah,' he replied.

I stammered that I was the navigator.

'Ah,' he deliberated, 'Geoff tol' me. I met 'im an' Frank an' Doog.'

He stared at me as though summing me up. I could not tell whether he was annoyed at being posted to our crew, or was slightly contemptuous of our inexperience. I realized later that it was neither.

He had begun his operations two years before we had begun ours, doing his first tour in Whitleys. I found later that his DFM had been awarded him after an operation on May 1st, 1941, when his crew had been caught in heavy icing on the way to Wilhelmshaven. Over the target Graham had succeeded in releasing the 500lb bombs by hand and had then been mainly instrumental in guiding the aircraft back to England in extremely bad weather. But of this we knew nothing until the war was over. We only knew that he had been involved in a shaky do over Wilhelmshaven, because he invariably showed a healthy respect for it whenever the place was mentioned as a target.

In the station church we had sung the first of the season's carols. The sermon being over, a quiet had fallen over those who had remained for Communion. As the Cup reached Jefferies, who was Bayliss's navigator, an amplified voice erupted at the other end of the room. Navigators were to report immediately to the navigation centre. Quiet settled again and the navigators left. Operations were briefed for Duisburg.

When the night came, it was moonlit with cloud piled to 14,000ft. We rode cautiously above it, silhouetted against its alpine surface, driven onward by a following wind. Over the Rhine valley the cloud broke and far below we saw our target. Two hundred and twenty planes were concentrated on a vicious city, but the flak was strangely restrained. Then about us we began to notice single vapour trails left by multitudes of fighters, described as though in chalk across the night. Somehow we bombed and turned away without becoming involved with them. Fourteen thousand feet below us Duisburg burned silently, the flames mirrored in the Rhine. Slowly the fires diminished behind us. The cloud was breaking completely, leaving forests, roads and blacked-out villages open to the moon. We left the coast, losing height slowly. With Doug at the controls Geoff came back to the cabin. He smiled enthusiastically.

'Bang on all the way! And how they pasted Duisburg!'

Then I began to realize that Duisburg might be our turning-point. A crew needed sufficient luck to carry it through its first operations, while it built confidence and skill. Though luck would always outbalance skill, a crew's first few operations required luck in a very large measure. After that, it could add to its luck a certain measure of skill.

The squadron had lost one crew, captained by Flight Sergeant Moriarty, a Canadian who had reached the squadron some time before we had ourselves. We lay in bed talking of him.

'He had bad luck right through,' said Geoff. 'Several times lately he failed to get off with engine trouble and now, when he does — '

'I suppose that's the way it goes,' I said.

'Yes; I suppose that's the way it goes.'

Two years later, when I was in Moriarty's city of Victoria,

I remembered having heard him say that his father was a journalist there. I called on chance at the first newspaper office I passed and there I found him, the older Moriarty, his dark eyes and his quick intense mannerisms so reminiscent of his son that I felt myself in the Lincolnshire mess again in the hours before take-off.

On the following evening we failed to get off ourselves on an operation to Munich. The blind flying panel of B was unserviceable and there was no reserve aircraft. As it was still early, I left the camp and stayed the night with friends in Scunthorpe. In the morning, when I returned, the crews were still sleeping after the operation, but Geoff was up and had left our room. I followed the road between the sports ground and the cabbage field to the crew room. No one was to be seen there, either in the room or on the tarmac where we usually paraded. I had turned towards the mess when I almost collided with Geoff. I was about to comment laughingly on his early rising when something in his face stopped me.

'Rose and Bayliss are missing,' he said.

We turned back down the empty road, walking without a word. Rose was an Australian Flight Lieutenant; Bayliss was Geoff's friend. Bayliss's navigator was Jefferies, an Australian I knew well; his wireless operator was Ian Robb, who lived near me in Australia.

We had returned to our room and Geoff was standing at the window, the familiar fire in him dead, when Doug came in.

He frowned. 'Rotten do. Something rotten for us, "Skip", too.'

'What is it?'

'The Wingco wants to see you — '

'Because we failed to get off?'

'Yes.'

This, we knew, was to be expected. The Wing Commander made it an almost routine affair to abuse captains who failed to get off, even if there were good reason for their failure. Perhaps he did it because he, too, was abused by those above him; perhaps he was afraid of the contagion of lowered morale.

'All right. I'll go while I feel like it.'

As the rest of the crew had heard this news, we went to the crew room together. After ten minutes of waiting there, Geoff came back to us, staring before him.

'Well?'

'I don't know how I stopped myself from punching his face.'

'What did he say?'

'That I was yellow; that we didn't want to get off; that he wouldn't have such things happening. I told him that our risks were enough without taking an unserviceable aircraft.'

'What did he say to that?'

'Raved and shouted and said he wouldn't tolerate lack of keenness. I asked him if he doubted the morale of my crew, and he began to cool down.'

We walked moodily down the road.

'Anyway, we'll be able to get away from the place this afternoon — we have a job to do in Yorkshire. Jock Greig was shot up last night and had to crash land at Topcliffe. They want us to pick up his crew.'

We reached Topcliffe by mid-afternoon. One of the runways was blocked by Greig's O Orange, which lay with one wing on the ground. We looked at the burnt-out starboard motor and saw the mark of flames beneath the wing. One tyre had been shot away and the rear turret was pock-marked with holes. The Canadian rear gunner had been wounded in the foot and was in the Topcliffe sick quarters. During their action a shot had somehow released the dinghy from the starboard wing. It had wrapped itself about the tail plane, increasing Greig's difficulties considerably. Lying there, broken, the aircraft told more of the past night than any words could have conveyed. It told of courage and comradeship and skill, but it told us, too, how thin a thread held us to mortal life.

Greig had reached Elsham with our draft, the only RAF pilot among us. He was now unshaven and obviously tired. He smiled at our congratulations.

'Ye kin thank the crew that we reached home at a'.'

We took the six remaining men aboard B Beer. Peter Bailey, the navigator, came forward and stood beside my table. He was a diminutive fellow from Yeovil, so neat and bright-eyed that he often reminded me of a robin. He waited until I had set course for Elsham, then asked how the rest of the crews had fared on the past night. When I told him who had gone his face darkened.

'There's not much future in Bomber Command.'

He stared ahead for a time, then climbed back to the rest position and lay on the bed. I left my table and went to the window. We were approaching the Humber near its junction with the Trent, the scene that of all English aerial scenes I recall most clearly. Below lay Reade's Island, the wide and muddy Humber flowing by on every side, and there, not far from the junction of the two rivers, the town of Goole. The Trent wound into the indistinct south, carrying my mind with it to Lichfield and the days of our training. Directly ahead, so skilfully camouflaged as to be scarcely discernible at all, lay Elsham Wolds. As we drew nearer I could see its runways, our barracks, the water tower and the mess. From 4,000ft in the Lincolnshire sky our squadron life, like the scene below, was something remote and unreal. Bayliss and Rose, the wide-eyed Kennard and the harassed Wing Commander were characters in a book read long ago and half forgotten.

We descended slowly, the Humber narrowing behind us. As the picture of Elsham clarified, the reality of our fantastic life crept back into my mind. I found myself looking at the small clusters of red-roofed cottages sprinkled across the wolds — Melton Ross, Kirmington and, a bigger, more congested cluster, Barnetby Junction. Warm red brick, nestling against the eternal green of England, they spoke eloquently of permanence and peace, the things we were so fast forgetting. I remembered the remark of a Scunthorpe woman, that she could not sleep until she heard us returning from operations in the early morning. On our way out and on our return, our engines would shake her walls and the walls of a thousand other cottages from Elsham to Mablethorpe. Sometimes as we peered down and saw only darkness, or a cloud floor, or an earth half-hidden by evening mists, my mind turned to the people of Lincolnshire, listening to the throb of our engines. Perhaps somewhere in the darkness between us our minds met theirs, for often as we passed overhead I felt them to be near us.

At dusk we landed. The narrow runway grew broader as we let down; the hangars, the watch office and the mess stood before us in their chill reality. Our squadron life now had neither remoteness nor unreality. There seemed, in fact, no other life; no other day than this day, this black day with its loss of fourteen familiar men, with its blot cast upon our name, with Jock Greig's broken Lancaster spread-eagled across that Yorkshire runway.

Everywhere carols were sung and that doleful tune, then so popular, 'I'm dreaming of a White Christmas.' So often did we hear it that even now its melody brings to mind the winter scene at Elsham: the snow banked about the walls of the mess; the metallic sky; the raw faces of people out of doors; the vapour of our breaths on the still air.

For Christmas Eve the sergeants had planned a ball, but when the day came we were briefed for operations to Turin. Graham Briggs dismissed this news with assurance.

'This 'appens every Christmas, but they always scrub it. The Jerries 'ave never come over 'ere, neither.'

Whether this was wholly true we did not know, but, accompanied by grumbling from the men, preparations for our departure continued.

A feeling that at some time probably attacked everyone, that night attacked me. Perhaps because it was the first operation after the loss of Bayliss and Rose, I felt certain, for no logical reason, that we would fail to return. Alone in our room before take-off I was placing together a few valued possessions when 'Chiefie', the LAC who swept our room, knocked discreetly and came in. He was a man of middle age, thin, drab and doleful, and plagued badly by 'the hashma'. He drew my attention with a wheezy cough.

'Off agin t'night, sarg?'

I answered him absently.

'I've set yer fire, sarg — y'll jist need t' put a match to it when y' come in.'

Having learnt to know this category of Englishman, I passed him a shilling, but my mind grasped the irony of his words, 'when you come in'. Indicating a pair of borrowed shoes to him, I said, 'If we don't happen to come back, would you mind sending these shoes to the address on the tag?'

He looked startled. 'You'll come back orright, sarg!'

'I dare say.' I was beginning to feel superior and to behave bravely. 'But if we don't, you'll see to these shoes, won't you?'

'Well, yes — o' course. But you'll git back, sarg; you're sure t' git back. You got a damn' good pilot.'

Although afraid, I was beginning to glory in my superiority.

'Rose and Bayliss were good pilots, too.'

'But Maddern'll get youse through. 'e's — 'e's——'

I left him lamenting over his broom. Outside the sun was already low. Every twig of the nearby wood stood motionless and sharply defined against a cloudless sky. I was aware that 'Chiefie' was behind me on the barracks steps, watching me get on my bike. I felt that something about me had convinced him that we would fail to return, as other men had imparted that feeling to me. I gave him a careless wave and rode towards the crew room. Out of the glare of the sun, which was setting directly before me, I heard a shout from Geoff, who was coming the opposite way.

'It's been scrubbed!'

I began to laugh. Geoff drew up and looked at me curiously.

'What's funny?'

'Nothing. Let's get ready for the dance!'

By nine-thirty Geoff was drunk. The crew thought this improved him, as he became unusually benevolent and produced from somewhere a charming manner. By ten his eyes had lost their usual fire and he had become exaggeratedly courteous. I watched him walk through the crowd carrying three empty glasses to the bar. Now and then he apologized gravely and profusely to someone he had happened to bump. The noise from the bar rose like the roar of traffic from a city street. As the sound of individual horns or the screech of individual brakes rose above the general roar, so a glass sometimes crashed to the floor, or a single voice rose above the roar of other voices. We breathed beer, tobacco smoke, hot bodies and hot pastry.

The bar was in the ante-room. Next door, in the mess itself, the orchestra played a tango. There was a slight haze of smoke in the air and a blending of perfumes. The Waafs were in a mood of excitement, more feminine beings than we had ever known them. I wondered that I was sober. There was a strange stiffness about my face, which did things to my speech, but my head was clear.

'Sober,' I remarked aloud. 'Absolutely sober.'

Geoff walked away from the bar with his three glasses filled. As I watched him he multiplied into three men who all began receding into the obscure distance. I touched Frank Holmes on the arm. 'Geoff is ver', ver' drunk.'

He thrust his face into mine. 'I think y' droonk y'self! Turn y' face t' the wall!'

I began an eloquent defence, but he interrupted it indifferently. 'Maddern's got two Waafs sitting with 'm — *two*!'

I focused my eyes on them. One girl I did not know, but I saw with a start that the other was Joan Sutherland. The distances clarified. I saw the curve of her cheek and the hair swept up from her collar. Geoff was expostulating with her gravely. She laughed and said something that caused him to throw up his hands despairingly. Then he began walking towards me. My mind cleared unpleasantly. I began walking towards the door, but Geoff arrived suddenly beside me.

'One of my frien's wants t' meet you. I warned her what you were like ——'

I said that I did not care to meet her.

'Don' talk bull!'

He grasped me by the arm and walked me to the table. While I stood there awkwardly, he began an elaborate introduction, bowing from the waist whenever the opportunity appeared to offer. I believe I sat beside Joan before the introduction was over. I did not look at her, but kept my eyes on Geoff and the girl beside him. Once I tried to tell Joan that I had wanted to meet her for a long time, but somehow the sentence was left unfinished. As soon as the glasses were empty Geoff picked them up and got to his feet.

'Gin an' lime for the girls and whisky for th' ole navigator an' me.'

I realized that I must drink nothing more. I asked Joan if she would dance, and while Geoff was at the bar we left the table. Even in my muddled state the full wonder of being alone with her suddenly struck me. I was hardly aware of our whereabouts, or of the presence of two or three hundred others.

We had been dancing for some time in silence when she said, 'What were you going to say?'

'Say?'

'You said it would be quieter here and we could talk.'

'I have wanted to talk to you for a long time — I'm not sure what about.'

'One morning we passed along the road near our barracks. You were about to say something then, weren't you?'

Almost forgetting her, I said, 'Munns; about Munns.'

I saw Munns' face very clearly — his greying, crinkled

hair and his tight mouth. "My only wish is to get the business over and get back to my wife and kiddy." And as I thought of him my mind cleared still more.

'Munns?'

'A navigator of our intake — he went with Winchester.'

'He was a friend of yours?'

'I hardly knew him. I heard him speak about his wife and child; then, a few days later, he was gone.'

I wanted to tell her how indifferent the squadron had seemed that morning; how I had felt that someone must say, 'This must stop!' But the dance ended. We walked back to our table, her arm against my hand. In the ante-room the noise had increased. A scarlet-faced warrant officer was attempting to drain a pint of beer at a gulp while fifteen or twenty voices shouted, 'Down! down! down!' A sergeant and a flight lieutenant wrestled absently in a pool of beer. At the table Geoff stood up and bowed elaborately.

'Whisky lined up for th' ole navigator an' gin an' lime for his partner.'

With a magnificent sweep of his hand he sent an empty glass crashing to the floor. It looked as though it would be impossible to escape and, besides, I owed him a round of drinks. I sat drinking cautiously, while we conversed in shouts above the general din. It was a Saturday afternoon in Perth and Geoff was sailing a yacht on the Swan river when I slipped away with Joan. We began dancing again and she began telling me of the Elsham Wolds of a year before. Then the squadron had been on Wellingtons and had a reputation for good luck.

'A lot of the boys who started together finished together — Holford, Johns, Pugh. Then the Halifaxes came.'

'Perhaps Lancs will be luckier.'

'Perhaps.'

'Or perhaps the ops are worse.'

'Sometimes I feel they must be.' We danced to a quieter corner of the room. 'When do you suppose it will end?'

'I try not to think. A few weeks ago I could do nothing

but think about things. Now I'm beginning to see that it's better to have nights like this.'

'Yes,' she said. Then, 'For us it's different. Perhaps if we ran your risks we could take this life as you take it. Some do, I know. Sometimes I wish I could, but suddenly I remember that some day it will end.' She added quickly, 'That's selfish, isn't it?'

'I don't know. When men are living our life it's hard for the women who have to live so near them.'

She said something that was drowned by the final crescendo of the orchestra. We walked across the floor, but instead of returning to our table we found a place on a form in the mess. The noise from the other room was reaching its climax in incoherent singing and the breaking of glasses. After the next dance Joan was to leave. Two gunners had drifted in from the bar and were dancing with each other, performing involved steps alone on the floor. The long hair of one had fallen across his face in an oily curtain. Every half-dozen steps he pulled the other up.

'Naviga'or, where are we? I'm flying blind.'

The other was pugnacious. 'Lis'en. I tole you b'fore, I'm not a bloody nav'gator, I'm straight AG.'

'Yo're naviga'or.'

'Say that again 'n' I'll 'it yer!'

'Yo're naviga'or.'

The navigator swung his fists wildly. The blows connected with nothing and he fell on the floor. As he lay there I saw him pick up a sprig of mistletoe. He regarded it tenderly, then struggled to his feet and held it over the couple sitting nearest him. The two kissed obediently. I saw before Joan did that he was moving our way. When she noticed him, I saw her colour slightly, but as he came to us she leaned towards me. He left us with her hand in mine, a sudden tension between us.

'Tomorrow I must thank him.'

'He won't remember it — and neither will you.' Her voice was unsteady.

'You are wrong,' I said.

The orchestra played again and we danced almost in silence. When the dance ended, Joan left for her coat. At the mess door I waited for her. The noise there had risen an octave in scale and was more meaningless than ever. Someone was attempting the old trick of walking on the ceiling and someone else, who looked suspiciously like Geoff, was biting off neckties. The far end of the room was obscured in a pall of smoke. I helped Joan into her coat and we stepped outside. The night was cold, but starry and very still. Instinctively we stopped and listened. Behind us an indistinct murmur came from the mess.

'This,' I felt, 'is reality. These stars and the darkness speak of things we must face.'

Beside me Joan was a shadow. I stooped suddenly and kissed her, as though, between us, all these things were understood. She said then, 'You see the way it is?'

'Yes,' I said. 'But you will come out with me sometimes?'

'Of course,' she said.

Before daylight on Christmas morning snow fell. It had ceased by the time we rose, but we walked to an early carol service over its virgin surface. Magor was at the organ, playing with his head tilted back, as though to enjoy more fully the music woven by his hands. We sang the last carol and filed outside, eyes puckered against the snow. About the horizon fog was forming, banishing all thought of ops from our minds.

An hour later I found myself in the warm embrace of P/O Brunning as the officers and sergeants walked to the airmen's mess to fulfil the tradition of serving 'other ranks' with Christmas dinner.

'My boy,' said Brunning, 'this is democrashy! This is the Chrishmesh spirit! This — excuse me, I doan' feel well.'

He fell face down into the snow and began moving convulsively.

'He's having a fit!' I said with some alarm.

'No,' said a Flight Lieutenant authoritatively; 'he's jush' swimmin' back t' the mess.'

As this seemed a reasonable explanation, we were about to leave Brunning where he was when one of his crew shouted, 'He can't swim!' This led a number of the braver souls to dive in beside him and render assistance. A motley group of waiters ultimately reached the airmen's mess to fulfil the tradition of serving 'other ranks' with their turkey and plum pudding.

In the huge cavern of the mess we heard cutlery clash with a noise like artillery. We breathed turkey, beer and pudding; we joined in singing the usual songs while the rows of airmen swayed in unison; we drank more beer. Soup was spilt, plates were broken, and unresisting Waafs were kissed with more ardour than Valentino showed at his best.

Like a spent storm the noise subsided. The airmen and Waafs trailed from the mess, leaving us shoulder-deep in washing up. As the day progressed, each gathering became confused with the one preceding it. Strange things began to happen. 'Blue' Freeman disappeared in the Wingco's car and was reported to have passed the guardhouse at seventy-five. Kennard took his crew somewhere in a jeep and while travelling along a road, ordered them to bale out. They obeyed him immediately, but someone landed on the W.Op. and broke his arm. A cyclist made a frontal attack on the MO's car and broke his leg.

By eight o'clock only the fittest were abroad. We prided ourselves on being able to cycle 5 miles to Brigg to visit Ted Batten and his wife, who were installed there at the 'Black Bull'. I remember that we sang something in the nature of carols and assured Ann that we would bring Ted safely through ops into 'the calm seas of matrimony'. At some unholy hour we left Ted and Ann on their doorstep. Still clutching 'Black Bull' tankards, we pedalled north through the fog. The last steep mile to the wolds forced us to walk, and not until the early hours of the morning did we fall into bed.

When daylight came the fog remained. All ranks of air crew were sent to the gymnasium and ordered into shorts and gym shoes. We stood huddled in a corner, shivering and blinking. A PT instructor danced into the room.

'Start running!'

We looked at him incredulously.

'I said, "Start running!"'

We fell over vaulting horses; we were knocked down by medicine balls; we clambered up bars on the walls.

'Faster! Faster!'

No relief came until a further casualty occurred. This man appeared to be seriously hurt — we even heard that he had died on the way to hospital. Later the report was modified. He had failed to see a vaulting horse and had done something to his back.

Outside there were seventeen degrees of frost. It lingered all day and, with it, the fog. Every blade of grass, every twig, every fence, was bearded with hoar frost. For several days this weather continued, appreciated only by Ted and Ann at the 'Black Bull'.

'30th December: The fog remains; the intense cold and stillness remain; the sun has gone forever. No ops now for ten days. This is not as pleasant as it sounds. Thirty ops must be done and, until they are done, the pressure is on. These long gaps give one too much time to think. We have still seen no one reach thirty.'

On one of these days I met Joan along the road beside the sports ground. I had begun to wonder whether she was avoiding me, but she approached smilingly. Her colour was heightened by the cold and the fog misted her coat. I looked at her with a strange feeling of incredulity, unable to believe that I had held her in my arms a few nights before.

'We are having a dance,' she said.

'On New Year's Eve.'

I thought she appeared disappointed. 'You have been invited?'

'No,' I admitted.

'Could you come, then?'

'Of course — if this is an invitation.'

The fog enclosed us so completely that I took the tips of her gloved fingers and drew her towards me.

'No, no! It's daylight!'

'I really did kiss you on Christmas Eve, didn't I?'

'I told you you would forget.'

I kissed her suddenly as we stood there, feeling the cold of her cheeks and warmth of her lips.

'You shouldn't. I've been trying to make resolutions — '

What they were I did not hear. Some of the crews came riding through the fog, breaking our isolation. I walked away, wishing Elsham life might go on unendingly. The unattainable thirty was something of no consequence.

I met Joan at the dance, but, perhaps by her manoeuvring, the evening passed without the lightest kiss. At midnight we joined hands for 'Auld Lang Syne'. Nearby I saw Syd Cook. My eyes happened to meet his, those courageous, confident, very boyish eyes. They said plainly, 'I wonder what 1943 holds? Already Col Bayliss had had it and we still have a long way to go.'

For Syd, could he have known it, the year held fifty more operations; a rise in rank from sergeant to a squadron leader of the Pathfinders; awards of the DFC and DFM, then death, death for the boy who had remarked to me on our arrival at Elsham that death was the only thing we had left to fear.

'If we can conquer that, we have overcome everything.'

Before he died he was to know that Col Bayliss was still alive. On his last operation Col's aircraft had been so crippled by a night fighter that he ordered 'abandon aircraft'. He was struggling to hold it steady for the crew to bale out when it exploded. Col was thrown clear; the others, including Jefferies and Robb, perished.

On that New Year's Eve these things were unknown to

Don Charlwood, RAAF

I

Peggy Forster and her van with (left to right, front) Geoff Maddern, Ted Batten, Graham Briggs and (at rear); W.J. ('Curly') Jones (visitor) and Doug Richards

Geoff Maddern and WAAF Intelligence Officer Lucette Edwards in the cockpit of Lancaster B-Beer

The five man Wellington Ic crew at Lichfield (27 OTU) in August 1942: left to right: Don Charlwood (navigator), Geoff Maddern (pilot), Ted Batten (bomb aimer), Max Burcher (wireless operator) and Arthur ('Shag') Browett (rear gunner)

Lancaster B-Beer W4333, Elsham Wolds, November 1942. The aircraft crashed on 5 March 1943

The enlarged crew in front of Lancaster B-B≈er, 103 Squadron, Elsham Wolds, November 1942; left to right: Arthur Browett (rear gunner), Doug Richards (flight engineer), Geoff Maddern (pilot), Ted Batten (bomb aimer)', Max Burcher (wireless operator), Frank Holmes (mid-upper gunner) and Don Charlwood (navigator)

Top: Ted Batten, RAF, bomb aimer
Left: Geoff Maddern, RAAF, pilot
Above: Doug Richards, RAF, flight engineer

Above: Graham Briggs, RAF, wireless operator
Top: Frank Holmes, RAF, mid-upper gunner
Right: Arthur ('Shag') Browett, RAF, rear gunner

Five of the crew of Lancaster B-Beer the day after finishing their tour; left to right: Geoff Maddern, Arthur Browett, Frank Holmes, Don Charlwood and Doug Richards

us. I left Joan outside the Waafs' mess, a slim, solitary figure in the fog. I walked up the familiar road to Elsham, past the beet fields, the haystacks, and between the darkened wolds. A feeling of depression was with me, begun perhaps by Syd Cook's unmistakable glance. I remembered again that no one had reached thirty ops since we had been on the squadron.

'Only three or four crews who were at Elsham when we came are here still — and these have been quiet months, interrupted by training and weather.'

Tramping the last icy mile to our room, I shook the mood away.

'Tomorrow we must operate. We have been waiting too long.'

CHAPTER SIX

Battle of the Ruhr

W ith the New Year the weather cleared, but there were no operations until January 4th. We prepared then to go to Essen. In the briefing room the crews went to their places and sat peering at the map of Europe. On it our route was marked with the usual lengths of wool and there was nothing to indicate that the night's operation was to be any different from those of other nights. Standing beside the map was a blackboard on which it was usual to show the number of 'planes being despatched from each Group in the Command. We were accustomed to read: '1 Group (our own) 140; 2 Group 120; 5 Group 150' and so on. Tonight we read: 1 Group 30, but before the other groups no numbers appeared at all. When the briefing officer entered the room, one of the men asked how many aircraft the other groups were sending.

He replied, 'So far we haven't received their figures.'

This reply satisfied us, but the truth was that no others were taking part. Bomber Command was experimenting with a new technique and evidently did not intend risking many aircraft.

The technique was this: Mosquitoes carrying special types of flares and markers were to precede us. By a method that could not be divulged, they would be guided to the target and would mark it for the aircraft following. If the night were clear, they would mark it with conspicuous red ground markers; if it were cloudy, they would drop a flare above the cloud, which would be so positioned that if we bombed it as instructed, we would hit the target.

We learned much later that the Mosquitoes reached the target on a narrow beam, directed from England. When they reached a radar-measured distance along the beam, a light in the cockpit warned them to drop the marker. This method

became well-known under the code name of Musical Oboe.
The Musical Oboe equipment was carried by a force soon
to become famous as the Pathfinders.

The thirty aircraft of the main force were to fly at
23,000ft, which was approximately double our usual height.
As the target was likely to be cloud-covered, it was expected
we would bomb a flare. This flare we were to approach at a
predetermined height and speed, steering a predetermined
course — matters carefully calculated by the 'boffins'. The
weather forecast was poor. On the climb to 23,000ft icing
threatened to be heavy. When we levelled out it would be in
a westerly wind of 110 miles an hour, in a temperature of
-30°C. A forthright talk was given by the Group Captain.
The operation was not likely to be easy. The experiment had
been tried by a small number of aircraft on the previous
night. They had suffered 16 per cent casualties, which was
over three times the normal rate. The cause of this increase
was not known.

The night, when it came, brought many unforeseen
troubles, some of them arising from the new methods of
attack. As a result, only half the aircraft reached the target.
Within sight of Essen we ourselves were in difficulties. By
some strange freak, the oxygen lead to the rear turret was
cut by the turret's rotation and at 23,000ft 'Shag' collapsed.
Then, in a dangerously long attempt to release him, Doug
came close to collapse as well. With the marker flares in
sight, we turned back.

But the attack evidently promised success, as we were
sent back, first in small numbers, then in hundreds. The Battle
of the Ruhr and the smashing of Krupps had begun. We did
not realize until long after that the tide of the aerial war had
turned. The cost in lives, even on our own small unit, became
appalling. Most of the familiar faces vanished from about
us. New men appeared, but we seldom learned to know their
names. Men fully trained on Lancasters began arriving from
the conversion unit at Lindholme, but often they did not have
time to unpack their kit before they, too, were lost. From

day to day we were seldom far from the station, but every six weeks we were granted six days' leave. To live until his next leave became the greatest hope of each man.

Our fourth month on the squadron passed, but no one reached the elusive thirty operations. Very few indeed reached ten. Each time we sighted the Ruhr we felt convinced afresh that to come through it alive was impossible. In the moments before bombing I stood, as hundreds of others stood, my heart booming above the roar of the engines, my chewing gum dry and tasteless in my mouth, my stomach contracted to a stone. I was conscious then of waiting for sudden oblivion. We were men before a firing squad of erratic marksmen. Kill us tonight or tomorrow night they might; kill us by next month they could scarcely fail to do.

Often the weather was so foul that ops were scrubbed, sometimes while we were waiting in the aircraft to take off. On these nights there were bigger and more abandoned crowds in the Scunthorpe bus and more hilarious parties in the mess. Though I was nearly always with the crew, these January days threw me, too, into the company of Joan. In the fantasy of squadron life she became something increasingly sane, a survival of the other life we had left behind.

In relationships between men and women, squadron life was a forcing house, not only in a physical sense, but in intimacy of companionship. A feeling of urgency seldom left us, so that a man would sometimes give his innermost thoughts into the keeping of a girl he had known for little more than days. If there were things on his mind that clamoured for expression, he would express them tonight, before the icy tramp back to the squadron for a late take-off, perhaps feeling that thus he was defying the oblivion before him. He spoke of love and war and death in strange places — in pubs, or in buses speeding for the nearest town, or sitting in some scantily sheltered spot in the open air.

There was something about Joan that would normally have forbidden quick acquaintance, but in those January days all barriers between us vanished. She left her past and her future and lived the squadron life of the present. I knew then that there were factors that made marriage between us well-nigh impossible. What those factors were no longer matters, nor did it seem to matter then.

Briefings continued at high pressure, and always we were briefed for the Ruhr. After a time the most timid of men can become accustomed to the most threatened of lives. We became accustomed to seeing planes disintegrate beside us and to learn on our return that in them were probably men we had known and admired; we even became accustomed to the idea that to reach thirty ops was no longer possible, that home was a place for which we could afford no longings.

'*12th January* — or two days before our leave. I hope to go to Somerset, to the home of Nora and Stella, who last knew me as a child in Australia. Now we are in the mess, waiting for a 3.15am take-off. There are still two hours to go. Here in this long, green chair sleep sometimes sweeps over me. I am in the far paddocks at Nareen again, lying against a log, eating my lunch. Nearby, my horse, "The Pig", is cropping at the grass, her bridle taken under her foreleg and tied to the stirrup. The ground before me falls to the Chetwynd Creek, then rises again to the tableland, where indistinct sheep huddle about the boles of trees. Even as I look at the familiar hillside, I know that I am not really there, that it is a place tantalizingly beyond reach. I wake suddenly to hear the rain that is delaying us lashing at the windows and to see the white-sweatered men lounging on all sides. Harry Wright is here, reading *War and Peace* with a furrowed brow; Brian Stoker, so much the English public-school boy, is speaking to the West Virginian, a fellow whose name has slipped my memory; others are asleep, all strain and fear smoothed from their faces —

Thou makest war to cease
Awhile, and armies pause;
And in the midst of strife
Thou bringest them to peace.

'Strange, this world of sleep. Even tonight as it envelops me, I feel myself embarking on subconscious seas, vaguely familiar from previous sailings. Things out of the past that I had imagined forgotten show themselves to be fully alive — happenings of childhood; emotions of long ago; things done that I have never considered since. Perhaps a time will come when the conscious and the subconscious will be one, presenting us with a treasury and a hell.

'To help fill a wait of twelve hours, many of us went to the cinema. We were treated to a film on road accidents in the "Crime Does Not Pay" series. As it ended a police inspector's face was flashed on to the screen.

'"Ah can tell you people in the audience that, at the present rate of road accidents, one out of every ten of you will be killed within the next five years."

'His promise I have probably misquoted, but it was sufficiently generous to rock the audience with laughter.

'Joan had come to the cinema with me. When it was over I walked to the Waafery with her under moody skies. The rain had not then started, but in the west dark clouds dominated the wolds. In the east, stars gleamed from the world we shall enter tonight. Joan's mood was subdued, the mood that rests on her frequently in the hours before ops. We walked close together, seldom speaking. Perhaps, if this were not ops life, I would have found myself drawn more strongly to her physically. As it is, the strongest need of her comes differently. It is almost as though we had been long married and had faced much together. I had imagined when we first met that it might be different; that, with the usual restraints missing, our emotions would have become more assertive. As it is, we kiss as those about to part kiss, with the unspoken realization that we are treading on the edge of the unknown.

'Tonight it was only 10 o'clock when we reached the Waafery. Instead of parting there, we walked on through the village. The clouds over the wolds had moved eastward, darkening the night and making individual houses indistinguishable. So far there was no wind. We climbed between blacked-out houses, each as silent as a hermit's cell. Once we smelt the baking of tomorrow's bread, then a cowyard, the cows stirring there and sighing. All the way Joan's shoulder lay against mine, but not until the village was behind did she speak. She said then, "I must show you the church the Saxons built." Not "the Saxon church"; but "the church the Saxons built", as though she herself had seen them there. She took me through a gate to high ground above the village. Of the church we could see little; rather we could feel it there, brooding on the rim of the wolds, looking out towards Elsham. On a neighbouring hill our beacon flashed its red characteristics, its clicking the only sound in the night. It momentarily inflamed a haystack and a cottage wall, then passed them back to darkness.

'I remembered that in seven hours I should be waiting for Ted to pronounce those blessed words, "Base beacon ahead!" The thought was strange. I pressed Joan's arm and felt her respond. We walked slowly down the hill to the Waafery in the face of a rising wind. At the gate we stood with linked fingers, the feeling of incredulity over us that always comes in these moments.

'With an effort I said, "I must go."

'Joan asked the question then that she always asks. "Are you in B tonight?"

"'Yes," I said. "Why must you always know?"

"'In B you are happiest —"

"'You ask because in the morning, when they say X X-ray is missing, or Y Yorker —"

"'No, you will always come back. Always," she said.

'I kissed her, feeling the rough material of her coat against my hands. The darkness suddenly engulfed her and Essen engulfed me. In a moment it was beyond belief that she had been so near.

'As I reached Elsham the front came with rain and wind. I retreated to this room, to the odour of beer and smoke and to the decrepit gramophone and its never-ending song, "How Deep is the Night".'

On the operation that night we had trouble with B's port motor. Early on the following morning Doug came to our room.

'It's on again — we're taking L London.'

'B is U/S, then?' I said.

He shook his head. 'She's fit to take. London is the Wingco's idea.'

Geoff sat up suddenly in bed. 'Throw me my clothes — I'll tell the Wingco we want our own kite.'

We found that B had been given to a pilot named Attwood, who was attached to Elsham from 12 Squadron for one night. It seemed probable that the Wingco had intended giving us the better of the two aircraft, but to us L London was unthinkable — in L we had been caught over Denmark and, in Halifax L, caught in the raid on Hull. The Wingco granted Geoff's request readily: Attwood would fly L London and we would fly B Beer.

Attwood travelled in the bus with us when we went to the aircraft. We sat opposite each other, the crew that was to have taken B and the crew that was to have taken L. They were complete strangers to the squadron and they sat saying little, even to each other. At 4.30 in the afternoon we started our engines. Doug eyed the sick port outer closely, but it sang its part full-throatedly. It was 5 o'clock and still daylight when we lined up for take-off. I stood behind Doug as we began our run. We were lifting off when the port outer stopped. Something fell away from it and at the same moment we heard a call from Geoff, 'Port outer afire?'

I saw Doug's hand go to the extinguisher button. B hung a moment, as though deciding whether to fly on or fling herself into the ground. Unseen by us, the Brigg fire brigade had turned out and was waiting for the fire to take hold. But the flames subsided. We climbed slowly out to sea, and 40 miles from the coast dropped the 4,000lb bomb. From the rear turret 'Shag' saw the sea tremble and subside. At 6,000ft B shuddered.

'Now we are taking this kite back — and we are not flying it again till it gets a new port outer.'

Some time after we had landed, I went to Barnetby and met Joan. We walked slowly across the fields to Melton Ross, sometimes startling sheep, so that they ran off into the darkness, their hoofs drumming on the ground. Before eleven we stopped and listened. In the east there was a murmur of engines that grew rapidly to a roar. The 'planes were returning, not singly but almost together. In the sound of them there was triumph, as though they cried, 'We have defied the worst and are still living.'

When I returned to our room Geoff was sitting moodily by our fire talking to Doug. As I came in he glanced up.

'Attwood has gone. L failed to return.'

We were silent for several seconds, then Doug said something we had forgotten in our moment of self-recrimination.

'I think it might have gone the same way with them if they had taken B. They wouldn't have been prepared for that port outer — we were.'

Geoff was poking at the fire.

'I suppose that's the way it goes,' he said.

'*14th January*: Outside all is quiet. A calm sea reaches to the Quantocks and beyond the Quantocks the sun has set. While Nora prepares tea, I am sitting in the kitchen listening to the saucepans bubbling on the stove, feeling content to have reached this leave.

'After lunch today Doug left Elsham by car for his home

in Cardiff. "Shag" travelled with him to Newark; Graham to Hinckley and I to Bristol. Beyond Brigg we joined Ermine Street, that straight road thrust into the north by the Romans. An avenue of trees led over level distances to the sky. At first I did not see at the end of it a distant pale glory of stone, standing over an indistinct city. As we drew nearer I saw a cathedral, like a crown on the head of the city. In its white walls every window glinted in the sun. Lincoln!

'Of such places is England made. Sometimes I find myself staring at them in wonder. Surely there never was a country like her! It is as though the spoken words of every being who trod this lovely way had enriched the English air. By the time I reached Burnham it was midnight. Now my first day is over, leaving five days stretching endlessly before me.'

In those five days I ate home-cooked meals, drank quarts of cider, lay long in my bath and longer in my bed. And I rode a bicycle along that enchanted coast from Bridgwater to Nether Stowey, to Watchet, Dunster and Porlock, descending at last into the valley of the Doones.

My last evening was a Sunday. As I walked home along the beach the tide was coming in slowly, sending subdued waves across the sands. A score or so of gulls rested with folded wings on the edge of the sunpath. Most of the people had gone home, but from somewhere I could hear the distant voices of children. The bell of St Andrews rang for evensong; a few gulls wheeled and cried; a light mist rose from the sea.

At breakfast I heard that there had been operations to Berlin with heavy losses. Before lunch I met Doug in Bristol. By the time we reached Elsham it was after eleven and very dark. At the gate we asked the one question on our minds. 'Who have we lost in the last six days?'

'No one,' said the guard. 'All back safe — even from Berlin.'

'Are they out tonight?'

'No, not tonight, sarg, but I 'eard they was nearly goin' t' send a few of 'em back t' the Big City an' then they scrubbed it.'

I went immediately to Keith Webber's room, feeling relieved and light-hearted. The men of his crew were our closest friends. Keith sat on his bed packing a canvas bag in preparation for leave. A well-stoked fire glowed in the stove behind him.

He looked up, smiling. 'Welcome back! — though I'd sooner be going than coming. How was the leave?'

'Perfect — until they broadcast the losses on Berlin. What was it like?'

He cleared some clothes from his bed and motioned me to sit down. I thought at that moment how old and tired he looked. I believe operational life was harder for him than for any man among us. Although he never complained and was a careful and exact navigator, I sometimes felt that he had seen into his own future and had realized that, whatever his ability, he was faced with impossible odds. Lately he had been unable to eat many of the mess meals and had become more stooped and greyer about the temples. But he remained the soul of courtesy.

'It wasn't as bad as we expected,' he said. 'A tremendous concentration of searchlights, but we've seen worse flak. I think it must have been a fighter night and we were lucky enough not to strike any.'

'What was the navigation like?'

'Fair enough. Beyond Gee range I found most of it DR. Radio beacons were jammed and we didn't care to steady up more than a couple of times for astro.'

He said then, 'By the way, they had a bad night at 12 Squadron — four aircraft lost out of six. I've been wondering how Col Miller and Wilf Burrows got on.'

These navigators were two of the Twenty Men. 'We'd better ring them in the morning,' I said.

But in the morning operations were on again and the

'phones were closed. Once again the target was Essen. Over Lincolnshire the morning was overcast but calm, the visibility clear. Ops appeared so certain that already the days at Burnham had receded far into the past. All my life I had been a navigator at Elsham, waiting for the time of take-off. At the crew room door I met Keith, dressed to go on leave.

'I thought you'd be down at the station.'

He shook his head. 'Our leave is scrubbed. We're going on ops.'

I stopped. 'What's the idea?'

He smiled wryly. 'The squadron is short of a crew. Roly Newitt force-landed after Berlin and hasn't been able to get back.'

'What does that matter? We could go a crew short.'

He shrugged. 'The Wingco seems to be able to find plenty of reasons. We aren't popular with him at present. Of course, we were off flying for a time when our W.Op. had measles, then one night after that we failed to get off. He hammered us about it, so I don't think Ted is keen to complain about tonight.'

Though I discussed the operation no further with Keith, the alarming feeling came to me that we were watching the last hours of his crew's life. I tried to cast the idea from my mind, but when I went to our room the feeling strengthened. Geoff was pacing the floor there restlessly. As I entered he exclaimed, 'It's wrong! Their leave is six weeks overdue.'

He did not so much as mention names, but when I looked at him I knew that he, too, was caught by the same irrational fear as I was. Although no one spoke of it until later, we realized that each man in our crew felt the same conviction, one of those irrational convictions that sometimes fastened on us in operational life.

I saw Keith next at navigator's briefing, stooped intently over his chart. As he had not previously flown on a high-level operation to the Ruhr, I went to his table with the idea of mentioning that the operation should be a reasonable one, as cloud cover was promised over Europe. When I spoke he was checking his tracks and distances with his usual meticulous care. As he glanced up I was surprised to see that his disappointment had vanished. There was more youthfulness about him than I had seen since we had left Canada, as though a conflict within him had suddenly been resolved.

'Now that we are this far,' he said, 'I don't mind it.'

They sat in front of us at main briefing: Ted Laing, plump and happy-looking, his complexion always glowing, as though he had emerged from a shower; Keith, stooped, serious and intent; Tony Willis, rosy-cheeked and black-haired. Again and again my eyes were drawn to them, to Keith's greying temples and to Ted Laing's fresh complexion. Ted in particular looked so vibrant that my forebodings were hideous by contrast. We did not speak again to them until the time came to drive to the 'planes. They were sitting in a small van, Ted Laing and Keith nearest the back. We exchanged the usual words with them, then they were gone.

At nine o'clock next morning I was awake. Between our curtains, beams of sunlight poured on to Geoff's bed. Geoff appeared to be sleeping, his blankets drawn over his head. I rose and drew back the curtains. The morning was innocently mild and bright. When I went outside I saw a party of workmen laying the foundations of new huts close to our own. Each morning for some days I had noticed them there. Sometimes I wondered what they thought of us, the wan, bearded, untidy-looking men they saw rising when half their morning's work was done. It seemed wrong on this morning that they should be there at all; wrong that they should appear to be taking life so much for granted. I felt an impulse to walk over to them, to say, 'I am sorry, but you shouldn't be here. The sane life of daily work has ended. You cannot have heard that Keith has gone, gone since you dug those holes last night, and probably we shall never hear of him again.' With my overcoat over my pyjamas I stood watching them, till one of them looked up and greeted me. I nodded vaguely, but did not speak.

A van drove down the road from Headquarters. Outside the rooms that Laing's crew had occupied it drew up and dropped two men. They vanished inside, reappearing after a time with personal belongings we had seen there a few hours before. Little of Keith's was there. When ops were announced he had arranged to have his belongings sent to friends. I went and dressed and set out for the ops block. On the road between the cabbage field and the sports ground I met Ted Batten.

'We're on again tonight,' he said.

'Same place?'

'Same place.'

I shrugged.

'Where are you going?' he asked.

'To the switchboard to 'phone 12 Squadron — I want to find how Col Miller and Wilf Burrows got on on the Berlin op.'

The LAC on the switchboard put me through to the sergeants' mess at 12. I asked if I could speak to either Sergeant Miller, or Sergeant Burrows, or any of the men from their crews. Whoever was answering said he was sorry. Both crews had been lost on Berlin. There was no news of any of them.

I walked away, past the mess, past the Gee room to the stores, remembering vaguely that I had to change an oxygen mask. Two girls I knew were sorting second-hand clothes on the concrete floor. I stood looking at the clothing.

'Fox, Morris, Winchester, Laing —'

I stopped this outburst ashamedly. A girl I did not know came from somewhere in the background as though to reply to me. Instead she said, 'You'll get through and you'll go back to Australia.'

The words were so unexpected and so absurd that I laughed. She looked at me steadily. 'It's true, I know it's true.'

I walked out, still laughing, but as I came to the road it

struck me that what the girl had said was true. Though I argued that this was mere superstition, the conviction lodged in my mind that some day I would return.

Along the road I met Geoff. 'The Ruhr again?'

'Was to have been. It's been scrubbed.'

'A girl in stores just predicted my future — I'm to survive ops and to return to Australia. How's that?'

'Fair enough — if I can come with you.'

'Funny how superstitious a man becomes. I had the conviction she was right, even though I knew we'd never seen a crew reach thirty.'

We had reached the mess. Though the bar was open, the anteroom was empty. We sat over a table drinking.

'I had a conviction like that myself one day,' said Geoff. 'I was riding over here from our room when suddenly I felt certain that we would get through.'

I let my mind toy with these flimsy promises, but slowly the full memory returned to me of Keith and Ted sitting together only twenty-four hours before. Their loss had been to me something different from all other losses, a sort of anaesthetizing against the losses that were to come and against many of the fears that had previously gripped me.

CHAPTER SEVEN

Target Essen

The ground crew have shut the rear door, sealing us within the fuselage. Down the long, dim interior I can see the bulkhead and the armour-plated door, then the stretcher at the rest position, then, in the empty, ribbed belly, the legs of the mid-upper gunner dangling from his turret. Beyond him, where it is too dark to see, sits the rear gunner, most isolated of us all.

It is five months today since we came to the squadron, sufficient time for us to have brought more detachment to these hours than we had imagined possible. For the fourth successive night the target is Essen; the time of take-off 1715. In the semi-darkness rain is pattering insistently on the metal shell encasing us. Through the wet windscreen the outer world is distorted as though by tears — its multitude of lights, its vague, squat buildings, its low-hanging cloud. As we begin trundling to take-off position the nearer lights assume a new order, forming a long line on either side of a straight, wet road that narrows in the indefinite distance and leads God knows where. Naked gooseneck flares are out, the flares that can best be seen in such weather as lies tonight over the whole east coast.

At the take-off position there is no waiting. The same words are spoken as on every night.

'You've got your green, Skipper.'

'Thanks, Doug. Everyone OK?' A pause follows that seems very long. 'Here we go then.'

Whatever we may be in other hours, in this moment of take-off, as we part from the earth, a different spirit holds us. In the voices that have spoken I could swear that there was a momentary realization, called out by the intensity of the hour. What the realization may be for each man, I do not know, but I feel that in it there is an awareness of his love for the men with him and, more than this, a moment of widened vision in which all danger, and death itself, assume their ultimate proportions, which are far less than the proportions we have given them in daily life. We feel on our bodies the forward surge of the aircraft and on our eardrums the assault of the engines. The instruments on my table begin vibrating as though in alarm. We lift from the earth; leave the lights; pass over the barracks. Behind us the flarepath shrinks rapidly.

I write, 'Airborne 1715.'

'Undercarriage!'

'Undercarriage!'

On the familiar order and reply Doug retracts the wheels. Obscure in the failing light I can see the village. Somewhere among the huddled buildings the girl of the fair, upswept hair is listening. That we stood so close an hour ago I can scarcely believe. We are in cloud; now out of it; now deeply into the main layer. We are wrapped about in mists that erase from our minds all sense of whereabouts. To me we have become nothing more than a mark on the white expanse of my chart, which we shall remain until the journey is over.

For a long time we climb on instruments until, at 10,000ft, the cloud about us is diffused with light. Like a diver rising from the sea, we emerge into a region of waning sunlight and clear skies. About us a floor of cloud is flushed by a sun that has not yet set. Arched above it is the dome of the sky, quickly darkening. In this Arctic region nothing else exists.

There is still half an hour before we set course. In this half hour the whole squadron must climb to 15,000ft, then set course over Elsham for Sheringham, the rendezvous. A second 'plane breaks through. Passing it we read its identification.

'K Kitty — Berry's kite.'

A third and a fourth 'plane rise from below us. Beautifully they bank and climb. Ted's voice reaches me, metallic on the intercom. 'There's a small break in the cloud.

I can see the Humber and Reade's Island. Now it's closing over.'

Against the roar of climbing revs our voices sound distant and unreal, as though, instead of sitting close together, we were separated by many miles in the outer emptiness. Out of the east night is rising, majestic and overwhelmingly lonely. Jupiter hangs pale above us. We are England's no longer, but creatures of the void. About the edges of our consciousness lap waves from our other life, memories of places and persons and spoken words.

Even as I glance out at the chill host of stars, I see with another eye the faces of those very far away, further away in time and spirit than the stars themselves.

'Can you see anything more?'

'Nothing but cloud.'

In the background of the intercom the note of base beam is guiding us on our climb. We remain on it to 15,000ft, the height of setting course.

'How long to go?'

'Five minutes.'

'Thanks.'

I fasten my blackout curtain and turn up the Anglepoise lamp. The outer scene becomes something unreal; the real world is this glaring chart with its bare outline of coasts and rivers. The Gee indicates that we are approaching Elsham, not the Elsham of the mess and the barracks, but an Elsham that is a spot of ink on the chart before me.

'Set course on 135 degrees magnetic in one minute.'

'OK. Set 135 on that compass, please, Doug. Check the deviation.'

A following wind is waiting to join strength with our engines in hurling us into the conflict ahead, as though they, not we were masters. While I listen for the words 'Setting course', as a sprinter listens for the starter's gun, my mind reaches out to tenuous links with the life we have left behind — an Air Almanac, published at His Majesty's Stationery Office; my cap, at the back of the table; a tin of orange juice from some Californian orchard.

'Setting course, navigator — 135 magnetic.'

B's leash is slipped and the game has begun ...

These moments before setting course were moments of waiting. Then would come the avalanche of work at high speed, the dodging of coastal defences, the ceaseless watch for fighters, the sight of the target in its unbelievable ferocity.

I would try to tell myself then that this was a city, a place inhabited by beings such as ourselves, a place with the familiar sights of civilization. But the thought would carry little conviction. A German city was always this, this hellish picture of flame, gunfire and searchlights, an unreal picture because we could not hear it or feel its breath. Sometimes, when the smoke rolled back and we saw streets and buildings, I felt startled. Perhaps if we had seen the white, upturned faces of people, as over England we sometimes did, our hearts would have rebelled ...

Geoff is searching for a way out. I go back to the cabin, fasten the blackout curtain and turn up the lamp. Before me the hand of the DR compass is progressing jerkily about its dial as Geoff makes his turns. After a long time I hear his voice, 'We're through!'

I begin to chew a piece of gum that has lain dry in my mouth and turn again to the chart. With dreadful slowness we begin moving across its white expanse. Astern, the target still appears within reach of our hands. These first moments of the journey home are moments of reaction; suddenly we feel overwhelmingly tired and indifferent to our fate.

'What do I want now? What do I want? A check on the wind; yes, of course, a check on the wind.'

But I sit motionless at the table.

Graham has begun to doze. I prod him with my long rule. He opens his eyes, his expression slightly startled, and changes his plug from the receiver to the intercom.

'What's the matter?'

'You had fallen asleep.'

His brow contracts angrily. 'Like 'ell! I was listenin'

out on base!'

'Oh, shut up you two!'

Graham changes plugs again, his eyes expressing injured virtue. Silence returns, except for the endless throbbing of the motors. Very deliberately Graham closes his eyes, but from time to time he lifts his hand to adjust his various dials and prove his wakefulness.

Hell, what does it matter, anyhow! For all the good I'm doing I might as well be asleep myself. I should take caffeine, but the tablets are in the bottom of my bag and the bag is under the table. Perhaps Joan is awake, visualizing me doing something heroic. Instead I haven't will-power sufficient to stand up and shoot a star. Joan with her hair about her face, her uniform laid aside ...

Nearly two hours have passed since we left the target. Now I can speak that comforting sentence, 'We have crossed the enemy coast and are well out to sea.' Everyone, I feel, has sighed deeply. The nose is down and the engines have taken on a note of contentment. Though danger has not yet passed, the tentacles of Europe have been loosened. We have set course for Mablethorpe, point of entry on the Lincolnshire coast. The cloud is breaking, sometimes revealing the face of the sea. Lights there flare up and fade, or flash urgently. Each night we see them and each night we wonder whether men are drifting there in rafts, or whether the enemy is trying to attract us low over waiting guns. The Gee is clarifying, making navigation easy and enjoyable.

'Three degrees east. ETA Mablethorpe 0025.'

Our evasive action ceases. As our height is now less than 10,000ft we unclip our oxygen masks and rub our faces; Geoff leaves the controls to Doug and comes back into the cabin. Clad as he is in his fur-lined jacket, his eyes narrowed against the lighting, his clothing exuding cold, he reminds me of a Wilson, or a Cherry-Garrard who has reached his base after a perilous journey. Although I have listened all night to his voice, I feel that we last met very long ago, when he and I were waiting together to face danger. Pulling off his gauntlets and the silk gloves beneath them, he clamps a pair of cold hands on my neck. I swing my elbow back. He smiles and prizes up the edge of my helmet with his thumb. Above the roar of the engines he shouts, 'You're lucky in here! It's dark and lonely out there.'

I shout back, 'That is all very well for the rest of you! I have to cross the coast at the right place, or we'll — '

'All right! All right! I'm going now.'

He presses behind me on his way aft, pushing my face on to the chart. He speaks to Graham for a time, then passes through the bulkhead door.

'Searchlights ahead. Looks like Hull.'

'Thanks, Ted.'

The beams appear relaxed and friendly, raised as though in languid welcome to the incoming crews. Geoff presses by again, coming forward. He passes out into the darkness and becomes a voice again. Graham asks the question he invariably asks, "Oo wants cawfee?'

Coffee is wanted by everyone. As I work out an alteration of course for Mablethorpe, Graham puts three flasks on the chart.

'Pass two up for'ard an' keep one for you an' me.'

'It's the same every night — you put bloody coffee right where I'm trying to work.'

'I could find the way 'ome from 'ere myself!'

'Alter course to 302 magnetic. ETA 0028.'

Always when I give this ETA for the English coast my tension is relieved and I know sweet satisfaction. Future danger does not exist. We have come through tonight; we have done what we set out to do; there are no men on earth better than these men beside me. I pour a flask of coffee and raise it to those in a family photograph before me. 'Another over! I'll see you yet!'

'Two beacons ahead — M Mother K Kitty and S Sugar R Robert.' I glance at the code list. 'Northcoates and Manby.'

'Ah yes, I can see the coast.'

We are at 5,000ft with only 20 miles to go. A milky sea

breaks on the coast below.

'If the Wingco had the sandra lights on we'd see the 'drome. No damned initiative, that's half his trouble.'

'There's the glow from the Scunthorpe steel works, Geoff. Base should be over to starboard.'

'Yes, OK, I see the beacon now. Shut up, everyone, I'll call control.'

The R/T clicks. 'Hello, Hazel control; B Beer. Over.'

A girl's voice rises to us. 'Hello B Beer, this is Hazel control. Pancake! Pancake! QFE one zero zero fife. Over.'

Sometimes I think of this voice as a symbol of the sanity and beauty we leave behind. There is a gladness in it and welcome — or do I imagine these things after listening for so long to the voices of six men?

The night becomes full of voices, each with its own accent and inflexion.

'Hello Hazel control; C Charlie. Over.'

'Hello C Charlie, this is Hazel control. Hold two thousand. Call funnels. QFE one zero zero fife.'

'Syd Cook. We've just beaten them in.'

'Hello Hazel control; K Kitty. Over.' The English voice of Ken Berry.

'Undercarriage!'

'Undercarriage!'

The wheels descend slowly.

'Flaps!'

'Flaps!'

'Hello Hazel control; L London. Over.' The Canadian voice of Roly Newitt.

'Start calling airspeeds, navigator.'

We are losing height rapidly, the engines throbbing in fine pitch.

'130, 125, 125 ——'

'Why the hell don't they change the runway. It's nearly cross wind!'

'120, 120, 115, 110 ——'

The wheels screech. We bounce and settle.

'Dreadful landin', Maddern.'

'Shut up!'

'B Beer, turn right at end of runway.'

We trundle among the patterned lights till a man appears in the beam of our landing lights waving us to our dispersal.

'Switch off!'

The song of the engines ceases. I slip off my helmet and rub my ears. Without the use of intercom I can hear Doug checking the petrol gauges. Geoff is impatient to be gone.

'Come on, navigator, let's get out of this damned thing! You're always bloody well last.'

'So would you be if you had all this stuff.'

'All right! All right! I'll carry your sextant for you. Not that I can see the sense in your taking the thing — you never use it.'

Frank comes forward, his face pained. '"Shag" an' me want t' get t' bed! Shoove the navigator's bag over, I'll carry it out.'

We scramble down the dim length of the fuselage to the open door. Oscar is there and Stanley, Bill Burchell and 'Misery', the men of our ground crew. Beyond them and all about them is darkness, still and very fresh. A bus with dimmed lights drives round the perimeter track to our dispersal. Peggy Forster, who always drives us, jumps out and takes some of the equipment from our hands.

'Good trip?'

'Very good.'

Geoff puts an arm round her shoulder.

'Thought you were off duty tonight?'

'Well, I was — sort of ——'

'Worries about us,' says Graham, 'that's 'er trouble.'

We scramble into the bus and drive on to K Kitty. The shadowy figures of Berry's crew climb amongst us.

'Good trip, Ken?'

'Oh, it's you, Geoff.' The voice is laconic and tired. 'Not bad on the whole. They hit us a few times — bomb aimer's got a splinter in the corner of his eye. How do you feel, Hop?'

'Quite OK, really.'

We talk half contentedly, half wearily, only the glowing cigarette ends marking our places. When we reach the buildings it happens that I go into the crew room alone. Five hours ago we stood here waiting and the room still seems to hold our suppressed tension, as though every piece of furniture and every diagram on the walls had absorbed something of our mood. The crew list for the night's operation is still in its place on the notice board, rustling in the draught from the open doors. Harry Wright comes in behind me, humming dolefully. We exchange a glance which says, 'So, we've done it again,' more clearly than words could have said it. Then Harry remarks, 'Young Morris isn't in.'

'Hell!'

We walk out together to the locker room listening to the few 'planes still overhead. The crew are waiting impatiently.

'Come on, let's get interrogation over.'

We walk out into the darkness again, our shoulders free of harness and Mae Wests. There are now no clouds in the sky and no 'planes. Someone asks if Morris is back.

'Not yet.'

'Christ!'

Our footfalls and voices echo along the corridor of the ops block. The ops room itself is filling with air crew, each man holding a cup of coffee and each talking light-heartedly. All are obviously weary, but release of tension has lent them a heightened gaiety. Overhead are the fluorescent lights, chill, dispassionate and shadowless. Two Waafs are serving coffee.

'Milk and sugar?'

'Thank you.'

'Good trip?'

'Wizard.'

Our eyes have been seeking for Morris's crew ever since we came in, but none of them are to be seen. Moving among the crews are the doctors, the padres, the Group Captain and the Wing Commander, men who never seem to sleep ...

Interrogation is over. We are in the mess, sitting to bacon

and eggs. There is fantasy in the conversation. We speak of the target, then of someone's shoes that need repairing, then of the 'plane that blew up near the coast. And we are thinking that Morris and all his crew are probably dead. Watching normal life flow about us, I marvel that our bodies continue apparently unaffected by the other half of our lives. We get hungry, we get sleepy, we see and hear and smell and touch everyday things as we have always done, but with the realization that suddenly we might never know these things again as we know them now.

Geoff and I go out together. In the enveloping darkness we stand and listen. There is no sound whatever. Something about the night overwhelms the senses. It holds a secret; it knows the fate of the missing crew, but it says nothing.

'There's no hope now. If they had landed away the ops people would have known.'

We walk along the road, wheeling our bikes, past the cottage that was once an isolated farm, through the white gate, past the cabbage field and the football ground.

'He was too young.'

'A bloody shame, a bloody shame.'

We turn then into our room.

By the end of February we were operating at high pressure. Essen, Dusseldorf, Wilhelmshaven, Nuremberg and Bremen were raided in a week. It seemed we would know by the end of March whether we were to reach the rest period that no one in six months had achieved. I saw Joan infrequently. Twice before ops I passed her on the road between the sports ground and the cabbage field and could only answer the question in her eyes with a nod.

The four senior crews on the squadron were unexpectedly posted to Blyton. A new Lancaster conversion unit had been opened there; but there was a shortage of instructors. As a result, Kennard, Berry, Douglas and Newitt and all the men of their crews were withdrawn from operations. Their totals ranged from twenty-two to twenty-eight. Kennard and Berry returned to Elsham a year later to begin second tours, but both were lost. Of the other two pilots, Douglas was also killed on his second tour; Newitt alone, the tall, blond Canadian, was to survive two tours.

Their departure in February left Austin the senior pilot, followed by Greig, Roper, Cook and Maddern. All these captains were sergeants, none of them with more than twenty operations, but soon after this Syd Cook was commissioned and, within weeks, had been promoted to Flight Lieutenant. Operations continued in rapid succession. We snatched sleep when we could, but for most of our waking hours a staring-eyed weariness gripped us and the pounding of engines was always in our ears.

As our tally mounted, Geoff's evasive action became increasingly violent. For hundreds of miles our bodies were compressed and extended by irregular changes of height. As my stomach had never responded cheerfully to 'weaving', it now rebelled completely. At first the nausea was confined to the air — a mere grabbing of a tin under my table; an attempt to conceal my shame and a few moments of incompetence. But as our periods of relaxation became fewer, last night's battering was scarcely over before tonight's began. At final briefing one night I mentioned it to Doc Henderson. He brought some pink powders from his bulging tunic pocket.

'Take these for the tummy.'

I drank them while he brought out some tablets.

'And these vitamins to take the place of last night's sleep.'

Lastly he gave me some caffeine tablets to take during the journey. I returned from ops that night with a settled stomach and wits so sharpened that my trouble seemed over. Doc Henderson looked closely into my eyes.

'When you get up this afternoon, slip round to sick quarters.'

We went to bed at 6.30am and slept for eight hours. When we rose it was snowing quietly, the sky banked darkly with cloud. The effect of the doc's drugs had worn off, leaving me dispirited and dull. At the sick quarters a number of air crew men, including Syd Cook and our own Ted Batten, were in bed. Rumour had it that the high-altitude work was taking more out of the men than had been anticipated and that each high-level operation was to count as one and a third. To my surprise I was ordered to bed. While estimating that at one and a third for each high-level trip we could add three to our total, I fell asleep.

I did not wake until the morning ritual of temperature taking. After this, Syd Cook and Ted Batten were discharged. Throughout the day I continued sleeping. In the evening a youthful Flying Officer came to my bedside, his hat under his arm, his uniform immaculate. I sat up abruptly, imagining that I might be dreaming. It was Max Bryant, my flying partner in Canada during the training of the Twenty Men.

He smiled, 'I'm posted here! Well managed, eh?'

'You asked for it?'

'*Asked*? It's taken me a month of begging and manoeuvring. The crew really weren't as keen as I was. You know, this damn' squadron of yours has a poor reputation.' He looked at me quizzically. 'Doesn't anyone ever survive?'

'Pugh and Johns, the Lichfield instructors, finished here.'

'In about 1066. No one since?'

'Four crews have just been posted as instructors to Blyton.'

'That's better! How long did it take them to reach their thirty?'

I became evasive.

'Did *any* of them reach thirty?'

'Very nearly. Anyway, if they let us off before we reach thirty, I won't be too proud.'

He made himself comfortable at the foot of my bed.

'How many have you chaps done?'

'I'm not certain,' I said. 'Thirteen actual, but rumour has it that high-level do's count one and a third, which would give us sixteen — just over halfway.'

'Fair enough — if it's true.'

'It won't be, but it sounds nice.'

'And what's it like here?' He looked at me intently, as he always did when he wished for the unvarnished truth.

'You'll like it,' I said honestly. 'It's different from the squadron life we were led to expect, but there *is* less bull and there *is* a different atmosphere about the place. Sometimes things get pretty grim, but there's something here that makes it all worth while.'

'I always did take those promises with a grain of salt. Anyway, the job's the thing. If I can drop a few eggs on Berlin —'

He looked at me and laughed. 'I sound like a sprog, I suppose.'

Having thought of him for so long as 'the gay crusader', I was about to dampen his enthusiasm, but I found that cynicism no longer came to me spontaneously. Instead I said, 'You'll need your enthusiasm. My trouble has been that I've never had enough.'

'You hadn't once. You have now, I think.'

When I thought of this, I realized that in part it was true. I still had little belief in the rectitude of our war or any other war, nor could I believe that more good than evil would arise from our mass bombing. That Keith and Wilf Burrows and Col Miller and now, probably, Max himself should die, was still something too ghastly to contemplate. And yet, on the squadron one could not for long admit cynicism, or pessimism, even in the face of the worst. Whatever my frame of mind had been when we had come to Elsham, I realized that now it had changed. Then I had been alone; now I had become one with a crew and a squadron. To demean them was impossible. So I said, 'You might be right. I don't quite know.'

Next morning was fine. Operations were to be to some distant target, but, as far as B Beer was concerned, another navigator was to take my place. As Geoff and I, alone of all the crew, had completed every operation together, the news cast me into despondency. When the doctor made his rounds

I asked to go. He eyed me dubiously for a time.

'Very well. I'll give you a few more of those powders before you leave.'

The target was Turin. For some months Italian targets had not been bombed, a fact apparent from the lack of the ice-cream cone symbol on the noses of our aircraft. The defences of Turin were known to have greatly strengthened, latest intelligence showing them to be approximately as strong as Düsseldorf.

We left soon after dark, a rising moon lighting the aerodrome. Moonlit England shrank below. The sinuous rivers; the lakes flashing under the moon; the dark fields; the black woods; the many wide-flung aerodrome lights; the indistinct towns; the winking beacons, all receded. Slowly the towns, the fields and the woods became one. The lakes and rivers fell into miniature, the moon still revealing them as they mirrored her light. Then they too became indistinguishable, leaving the aerodrome beacons alone flashing red and white, far away. It seemed to me now that all my life I had been sitting at this same green table, staring at this chart; that always my family had been people in the picture that stood before me; that my life-long companions had been these six men, their phlegmatic voices and the endless song of the engines the only sounds in my ears. Always our harness had been heavy; always the cabin had been stiflingly hot; always I had been flung across the green-topped table and back again. And always Death had been at our shoulder, so familiar a being that even he had become less feared. Only he could ever end this strange existence. Slowly the glitter of waves breaking on the English coast was lost in darkness. The deep silence, broken nowadays only by necessity, settled over the crew ...

Four hours later we were losing height and had begun weaving again. Turin lay ahead, marked by a tall cone of searchlights. For the first time the cloud below was breaking, revealing forested foothills, clear in the moonlight. As the first aircraft neared the target the cone sprang angrily into action. At the same time the air was filled with the smoke of shells. But when the first bombs fell, a strange thing happened. For a few moments the searchlights sought for aircraft, then, as though the defenders had been called to some more urgent duty, the beams stopped moving. Some remained pointing upward, some at acute angles, some almost horizontal. The whole scene had taken on the immobility of a picture. At the same time the flak almost ceased. We looked down incredulously. Under the light of the moon the city was mercilessly exposed — houses, churches, gardens, even statuary along the streets. The crews wheeled and dived, exulting as the Germans exulted over lightly-defended Britain in 1940. And yet, perhaps the minds of the attackers would have been easier if the Italians had attempted to defend their city. As it was, we blew women and children to pieces, unopposed by their men.

We turned away, back towards Lake Anisee, leaving Turin a torch behind us visible for a hundred miles. I took only one astro fix on the 400-mile leg, but for the rest of the journey had to depend on dead reckoning alone, as there was cloud above and below and the Gee was jammed. The one fix showed us to be south of track. I made an alteration of course, an alteration that proved by no means big enough. Once certain that the Alps were behind, Geoff resumed his evasive action, at first gently, but soon viciously. Again and again I scanned the screen of the Gee. It flickered, pulsated, shrank and swelled, but refused to yield a fix. For half an hour I stared into its green inferno, till nausea lingered about my throat.

'I must turn out the light. I must turn out the light, or by the time we reach the coast I shall be sick and useless.'

But the knowledge that those outside had no opportunity of relaxing probed the remnant of my conscience. Though I did little, I fought to remain awake. We dragged across the dazzling expanse of chart. Below us was unbroken cloud, concealing every possible pinpoint. Twice more I attempted to read the Gee, but was forced to grasp the tin under my table. I rested my head on my arms and felt relief creeping over me. The roar of the engines became like distant surf.

A voice roused me suddenly.

'No, it's not land. It's still cloud.'

'It's not sea, is it?'

I looked at my watch aghast. The time was 0350. The last entry in my log was 0346.

'No, it can't be sea — we're not due over the coast for nearly half an hour,' I said.

'It looks damn' like it and there's not a bit of flak about.'

'No,' said Geoff with certainty. 'It's a thin layer of cloud and we can see the ground through it. It looks as though we'll soon be able to pinpoint.'

'Good.' My throat was dry.

I turned to the Gee. The jamming was still intense, though I knew we should be very near the coast where a fix was normally possible. The gunners began calling flak, first at odd intervals, then frequently. Failing in all else, I asked for a fix as a check for crossing the coast. Graham tapped at his key, then held it down for fifteen seconds, transmitting the dash on which the direction finding stations would take their bearings.

The fix came back quickly and at the same moment Doug cried, 'I can pinpoint on the coast.'

At a glance I saw that the fix was marked 'Third class.' I said to Doug, 'Where do you think we are?'

'South of Le Havre — coming out just where we went in.'

I began plotting the fix light-heartedly, but it showed us at the base of the Cherbourg Peninsula. I asked Doug to look at my map and try to identify what he saw. At the same time I warned the crew to watch carefully ahead. Doug pushed aside my blackout curtain and stepped into the light, his eyes puckered. Stooping over the topographical map he placed his finger at the mouth of the Seine.

I called Geoff. 'Turn on to 319 degrees magnetic for Dungeness.'

He repeated the course and swung starboard. Within seconds the Gee clarified. At the same time Geoff called sharply, 'An island straight ahead!'

Without plotting a fix, our position was evident. I exclaimed, 'Guernsey! Turn out to the west!'

'It's a bit late — we're just crossing the coast.'

'Shag' stifled a yawn. 'Don't worry. They've only got old Jerries as gunners 'ere.'

As he concluded this remark, carefully predicted flak enclosed us in a square. Geoff flung the control column forward, pinning Graham and me to the roof. The airspeed indicator swung from 200 to 250, 300, 350. The flak rumbled beneath us, tossing us like a canoe in rapids. But Guernsey is small and our actual speed was over 400mph. Very soon it fell behind, its guns still tracing patterns in the sky.

As I relaxed, Geoff called, 'Another island ahead!'

'There can't be. You're probably looking at cloud.'

'I've never seen a cloud with lights on it. It's an island, I tell you.'

I plotted another fix. 'You're right — it's England.'

CHAPTER EIGHT

Wilhelmshaven

The valley of the Rhône passed beneath us, casting us into silence. The moon revealed peaks and glaciers, the course of the river, the villages in their valleys. In all the scene there was no sign of life, no movement, no lights, no smoke from chimneys, only the Alps hooded and cloaked with snow. When we looked directly below they appeared to pivot about their peaks, until I felt we could see the earth itself rotating. In the aircraft the moon showed Geoff clearly, his eyes narrowed above his mask, his helmet gleaming, his Irvin jacket with its collar upturned. Seeing him thus was to see the Geoff of Essen and Bremen, but when he spoke, his words took me unawares, 'Bombs should never be carried over a place like this.'

We were on our way to Milan and were off track in Swiss territory, a fact which would have to be confessed on the morrow, so that an apology could be sent to the Swiss Government. Again the Italians left their guns. The only heavy defences we saw were at Turin as we passed north of it. Although the city was being molested by no one, the gunners poured shells into the unoffending sky.

Powdrell's crew failed to return. Powdrell was a Squadron Leader who had replaced Fox. We heard much later that he had been hit by bombs from another of our 'planes.

'So ends an amazing three weeks — three weeks without a loss. It had given us an opportunity to get to know most of the men in the mess, but now the spell has broken, as all such spells must. Our photo of Milan last night was best for 1 Group and second best for Command. We happened to get a line overlap, a clear series of three photographs including the point of aim. It was op number seventeen, leaving thirteen to go. Austin, with twenty-four, now has the most senior crew. He is a likeable fellow — short, plump, rather pale, with straight, black hair that often falls across his forehead. He has brown eyes and the casual manner that often accompanies them. Somehow his battle dress looks slightly big for him. Perhaps it is the way he walks, his gait being almost as sloppy as Geoff's. A few nights ago he surprised me. Ops were scrubbed and, hearing someone cursing in the approved manner, he remarked, "Never curse a scrub. It might have been the op you were to go missing on." With the end of a tour in sight, many men would adopt the opposite attitude. Probably his crew will be the first we'll see reach thirty.'

By now Max Bryant had done his first operation — an attack on the submarine pens at Lorient. It happened that at this time 'Blue' Freeman was in disgrace. Twelve of the Twenty Men had held a reunion at a Doncaster hotel. 'Blue' had finished the evening with one of the best fights of his career. Unfortunately his opponents were local policemen. As a result of this, he lost his crew and, when Max came to operate, he had become a freelance navigator and bomb aimer. He flew with Max as a bomb aimer on the Lorient operation, their regular bomb aimer being ill.

By such pieces of voluntary operating, 'Blue' did half a tour. By his indifference to danger and his ability to fly in any of three or four different positions, he moulded many novices into good crews.

Max's tally of operations mounted rapidly. By mid-February his crew was off 'easier' targets and was ready to operate with the squadron proper. Twice then we were briefed for Wilhelmshaven and twice the operation was cancelled. Though news of the previous briefings had probably reached Germany, we were briefed again for the same target on the third successive night. All day heavy mist had limited the horizon, shutting out the wolds and causing a constant dripping from the trees. By evening it had closed in further, leaving the runway a road into nothingness. While we sat in B before take-off the junior crews were withdrawn. The Wing Commander's car pulled up then below our nose.

'Maddern, this weather threatens to get worse. Will you chaps volunteer to go?'

Over the intercom we heard Geoff mutter, 'A great way to run a squadron!' But through his window he shouted, 'OK sir, we'll go.'

I heard a murmur from the rear turret, ''Eroes, that's what we are! Tomorrow we'll all be wearin' gongs.'

But again the operation was cancelled.

Next day we were briefed for Wilhelmshaven for the fourth time. This time we got off.

'Where are we, navigator?'

'Over midway across the North Sea — 7° east. ETA Point X now 2205.'

'Thanks.'

To reach Point X on ETA, that is my sole ambition. Beyond Point X my mind does not reach. That is the turning point for our final run to the target. I remember a night over southern Germany when the Pathfinders were to lay yellow flares at just such a point as tonight's Point X. They were to lay them at 0130. At 0122 Geoff asked, 'When are those flares to go down?' '0130,' I said. 'You're sure of that?' 'Yes,' I said. 'It's bloody quiet round here.' Doug added, 'I haven't seen another kite for an hour.' The rest of the crew were accusingly silent. Until then I had worked confidently; now I began to have doubts. 'Any hope of a pinpoint, Ted?' 'No,' he replied, 'we're still over that sheet of cloud.' Silence again. I worked back over my chart; re-computed winds; re-plotted fixes. 'Navigator, I make it 0127 and there's not a sign of those bloody flares. No other kites about either,' added Doug again. A hand seized my throat. I muttered something about making another check, but I felt as if the aircraft were a runaway horse and I had lost both reins and stirrups. 'Still cloud below.' It was now 0129. We must be miles out. We could be over the Mediterranean. I picked up my computer and gazed at it for several seconds. A shout startled me, 'There go the flares!' Then Geoff's voice alone, 'Dead ahead, navigator. Nice work!' 'You bastards,' I said.

That was a long time ago. Tonight the Gee is working beyond its usual range and navigation is simple.

'What's that noise?'

'Ice breaking off the props.' It crashes along the fuselage.

B is climbing sluggishly, sheathed in ice. The crashing comes again, hollow-sounding on our shell.

'If there are any Stirlings on tonight they'll end up in the drink — they'll never top this stuff.'

'I believe the cloud is thinner above us.'

'Yes, that could be moonlight.'

'Where are we, navigator?'

'Five minutes from Point X. We're a couple of minutes early.'

'Thanks.'

'That *is* moonlight, Skipper. We'll be clear in another minute.'

'Good!'

We emerge from cloud into the amphitheatre of the sky. The moon rides above a white floor, paling the stars. Ahead the cloud is breaking.

'Navigator, I'll get rid of that two minutes with an orbit. It's clear enough to do it.'

'OK.'

I feel B turning to port. She is sluggish still in her cocoon of ice. The moonlight glitters on her wings.

'Fighter climbin', port quarter up! ME 109.'

I stop working and listen. 'Shag' is panting into his microphone as if he had run a long way.

Geoff's voice: 'Jettison cookie!'

'Bomb doors open!'

B leaps upward.

'Fighter comin' in! See 'im, Frank?'

'See 'im, "Shag"!'

'Prepare to turn port!'

Our nose is down, but the protecting cloud is now far below. 'Turn port, go!'

The airspeed indicator begins turning clockwise, 200, 250, 300; but even without the 4,000lb bomb, B is sluggish. Over the intercom comes the deathly chatter of our guns.

'Just missed us!'

"e's breakin' off, Frank!"

"e's comin' in again! Keep turnin', Geoff.'

The firing again; a long burst from both turrets.

"e's on fire!"

'Got the bassted!'

The fighter comes within sight of the cockpit. 'Good work! He's dropping into the sea!'

The floor of cloud reflects a sudden glare, then the fighter is swallowed up and the night is as before, clear, moonlit and empty. I find that I have been pressed against the wall behind my chair by our violent turn. The pressure eases; I take deep gulps of oxygen; I pick up my chart from the floor.

'Good show, gunners!'

'That damn' fighter was waitin'.'

'Too many Wilhelmshaven briefings.'

Perhaps it is so. Perhaps through the secret channels of the land below us the message has gone, 'Wilhelmshaven tonight, attacking from the north.'

I wonder how many German lives the dead pilot saved. He forced us to drop our main bomb into the sea and now he is beside it.

'It's hardly worth taking these incendiaries alone.'

'Bad luck, Skip. Might's well drop them, though.'

'There goes the flare!'

'Nice work, navigator. We'll keep away from it, eh? Might be fighters round it.'

Perhaps George Loder of the Twenty Men has dropped it. George, the Imperturbable, the Pathfinder. I remember him climbing Ben Nevis in a violent rainstorm. He was somewhere behind me, because I was walking quickly, in a fit of anger. If George and Harry insisted on climbing in weather like this, then may the heavens burst! High above Glen Nevis we paused and George confronted me, dye from his cap running down his face. 'Is this your usual pace up mountains?' He spoke mildly, but determinedly. I smiled and relaxed. We walked on then unhurriedly. The rain turned to snow, but suddenly, near the top, the cloud fell back and there below lay the Great Glen. Now Harry Waddell was dead. Perhaps George it was who dropped the flares.

'The cloud is breaking. I can see the Wilhelmshaven searchlights on the horizon.'

'Thanks, Ted.'

There must be others from the Twenty somewhere close by; almost as close now as they were in class; doing the same things here as they did there. Max Bryant is here and probably Bill Charlton, 'Tib' Barker and Johnnie Gordon. They twirl the face of their computer; they stare at the screen of their Gee; they plot each course meticulously.

'Enemy coast coming up.'

I turn out my light and stand behind Geoff and Doug. Ahead is a forest of searchlights, moving ceaselessly. To enter it is to walk with death. We do not go to cities, we go always to this forest. It lies at the end of every journey. Once Johnnie Gordon went to Germany with a new crew. When they came in sight of the target they were dumbfounded. They said to Johnnie, 'What's this going on ahead?' He looked out from the cabin and said, 'That is the target and the sooner you get in there the better.' I feel a little incredulous each time I see it. I cannot believe that any of us will emerge from it alive.

'Course out, navigator?'

Always before we enter the target Geoff sets the next course on his compass, in case in the confusion of the attack a mistake is made. I pass it quickly.

'There goes the Pathfinder marker!'

It falls to the ground and lies there, blood red, marking

the place we must bomb. It lies like an exposed heart. The flak has started in its streams of red, yellow and orange.

Beside us a Lancaster is heading into the target, a silhouette against the searchlights and the incendiaries spangling the ground. Her movements appear unhurried and confident, but as I watch, a blue searchlight snaps on to her, fastens on like a dog. The Lancaster swings to starboard, but a dozen other beams spring up and pinion her.

'They're coned!'

'We'll run in while those searchlights are occupied.'

The Lancaster has swung away from us. She is silvered by light and appears like a moth plunging at a candle flame. Shells are climbing unhurriedly into the cone of searchlights and bursting there, orange and black. Seven men are sitting on thousands of pounds of explosive and there is nothing we can do for them. Perhaps later they will be able to say, 'Over the target we were coned — had a hell of a job to get out of it.' Or perhaps tonight —

'They're hit!'

A flame, a little flame, at the root of their wing. And the shells are climbing still.

'Twelve seconds for a shell to reach twenty thousand feet.' I repeat to myself. 'Twelve seconds for a shell to reach twenty thousand feet.'

'We'll start our run in, Ted.'

'OK. About ten degrees starboard on to our heading.'

The little flame is growing.

'He's hit again — near the rear turret,' I say.

'Quiet while Ted runs in.'

'Further right, Geoff.'

Geoff kicks B round.

'Coming along nicely now.'

A parachute opens under the nose of the Lancaster and a man dangles there in the light. I look closely, but no more men appear. The aircraft begins dripping with red fluid, like blood.

'He must be a Pathfinder. His target indicators are

running out of him!'

'Shut up!'

'Left, left. Hold it steady now.'

Still no more men appear. The propellers are turning, but the Lancaster could be a ghost ship, her crew dead. But no, she turns a little, first one way and then the other.

'Steady, steady.'

A brilliant flash and she has gone. Now I can see nothing; no fragments; no smoke. The man on the parachute has vanished. Seven men are dead. The searchlights swing away and grope in our direction.

Huskily from the rear turret, 'Searchlight on our tail! Hurry it up, Batten!'

'Left a little. Good! The target is coming down the drift wires nicely.'

'Bloody lot of trouble for a few incendiaries!'

'Shut up!'

'Flak dead below us!'

I hear the crumpf! under my feet, then a quick series — crumpf! crumpf! crumpf!

'Steady! Steady! Bombs gone!'

I go back to the cabin and write it down, 'Bombs gone' and in the Remarks column: 'Lancaster at approx 18,000ft hit by flak, exploded. Appeared to be carrying T/Is. One man got out but disappeared after explosion.'

'Hold it steady for the photo.'

We are over the striking point of our bombs.

'Searchlights again! Blue bassted right in my face!'

An explosion swings the whole fuselage to port. Through our masks we can smell cordite.

'Steady a couple more seconds. Steady! Steady! Steady! OK Geoff, all yours.'

'Turning out, navigator.'

Below us the city is dying. Its searchlights still seek us and its shells still explode, but its streets and houses and hospitals and factories are an inferno. As we watch it is suddenly no longer night. For an instant day has come with a light day never had. The harbour, the city, the swarms of attacking 'planes, are printed on our eyes. Then it is dark again.

'Log that explosion, navigator. Must have been a gas works or a mine dump.'

We are out again, the sea below. I find my mouth is dry and my body suddenly exhausted.

'ETA Mablethorpe, four minutes after midnight.'

I went next night to Cleethorpes to stay at the 'Rookery'. I had tuned to Breslau, to 'The Marriage of Figaro', when the Cleethorpes sirens began. In the distance I heard the guns along the Humber, like a roll of drums, moving closer. Then they opened up somewhere behind the house, shaking the walls with each roar. I went to the door and looked out. The Hull searchlights had illumined the garden strangely with a bluish, ever-moving light. High up, I could hear the drone of an aircraft, tortured and afraid. Knowing only the terror of air crew, my heart was with the pilot carrying out his lone task against extreme odds. I saw his aircraft caught by the searchlights. Small as a moth and beautifully silvered, it dived and turned frantically, the flak growing rapidly closer. Though I could not see the end, it came soon. Searchlights were doused, the firing ceased, and the long cry of All Clear came from the sirens. I went inside and resumed listening to Mozart, wondering what manner of man had died.

When I returned in the morning, preparations for ops were already under way. The target was to be Bremen, the first target we ever visited in Germany. For us it was to be No. 20. We took off in fog and were subjected to the most intense flak we had so far seen, but not one aircraft out of the hundred sent failed to return.

With only twelve hours left before going on leave, we were briefed for Hamburg. Out of doors a deep quiet rested over the station. Though the evening was cold, scarcely a breath of air met us as we walked to the mess. On horizons usually limited by mists we could see cottages and individual trees. High on a radio mast, a blackbird sang from an overflowing heart. Watching and listening, I felt myself lulled into serenity, the feeling upon me that death itself could be nothing more than the breaking of the thin shell that bound us. Outside the mess, Peter Bailey hailed me.

'A scrub! It's just been announced.'

'So we get our leave!'

'Lucky men! Perhaps when you get back we'll be top crew.'

This was probable. Peter, being Jock Greig's navigator, had already reached twenty-two ops and had some time yet to operate before he went on leave. As his home was in Yeovil my enthusiasm for Somerset always pleased him. He exclaimed now as we parted, 'Whizzo for Somerset! Next time I'm home we might even have finished.'

Bill Charlton, another of the Twenty Men, was staying at Frome. We met one morning at Wells, below the west front of the cathedral. I recognized him from a distance, a tall, angular figure, pacing intently about the lawns, his hands clasped behind his back. He might easily have been a curate in RAAF uniform. When I saw him more clearly, I felt that Air Force life had probably changed him less than any of us. In repose his face was still serious, almost ascetic; in conversation he still gave the impression of being about to share some tremendous joke. He extended a large hand to me.

'It must be six months since I saw you! How many have you done?'

'Twenty,' I said.

'A gen man! You must give me a few hints.'

'What rot! I hear you turned on quite a performance not long ago.'

'No, no! Dave White, our skipper, did. They gave him an immediate DFC. I just sat in my chair — it had nothing to do with me.'

Dave White was a pilot who looked as if he should still have been at school.

'What happened?'

'Oh, a fighter — you know the sort of thing: blew out an engine and made some holes. Really, I didn't know much about it.' He changed the subject adroitly. 'How is Max Bryant coping?'

'Splendidly. He's had some shaky trips, but he's still full of enthusiasm.'

'He'll never lose that.'

We walked across the lawns still talking, looking absent-mindedly for a Cheddar bus. Our plan was to wander about the gorge and return to our Somerset homes for tea.

The gorge proved vaguely unsatisfying, but I shall always remember Cheddar with affection for the out-of-doors day it gave me with Bill. We left the road and climbed steep slopes of grass and rock, talking in panted sentences of the Twenty Men. The sight of Bill brought back their days in Canada, the cracking pace they set in class and in the air, and the close comradeship of them. And I saw Bill studying again, sitting up later than any of us, learning every detail slowly and thoroughly. He was wearing himself out, but his good nature seldom varied. As far as the future was concerned, I could see again that there was no romanticizing in him. Our task was distasteful, but we had committed ourselves to it. And again I could see him, between concern and laughter, saying:

'You know, I don't think I'll ever make a navigator.'

Now he climbed slowly, his angular figure stooped, his large hands illustrating every point he made as he spoke. I remembered how greatly we had admired him for his persistence in continuing to fly when he was so frequently racked by air sickness.

'Does air sickness still trouble you?'

'I'm afraid it does. Sometimes I feel it might be fairest to the crew if I pulled out. And yet, I wouldn't like to give up.'

'Does the doc know how bad it is?'

'I don't suppose he does. You know what it's like —

once you're on the ground you forget and you're willing to go again. Anyway, I've managed fifteen, so I suppose I'll manage more.'

We had risen above the protecting walls of the gorge, exposing ourselves to a wind from the north-west that scattered flurries of rain. Beside us climbed a fence, painstakingly built of stones gathered long before. At the top of the hill we sat on it, breathing heavily. After a time I saw Bill smile suddenly, 'Do you ever hear of Johnnie Gordon?' he asked.

Understanding his smile I said, 'Not since he was "billeted out among the reluctant Welsh people".'

Bill laughed. 'What a puzzle he was to me when I first met him! He told me his civil occupation was a burglar.'

I visualized the tall school teacher; the scholar of Latin and Greek, who read *Oedipus* and *The Medea* because he 'liked the murders in them'; the accomplished violinist who 'knew nothing about music, but enjoyed the noise it made.' The lonely man, introspective and moody, who rocked the Twenty Men with laughter.

'I must write to him,' I said. 'He was posted to Lancasters at Bottesford.'

Bill said, 'I've always remembered the day we were presented with our Wings. There I was ready to go on parade feeling very proud, while Johnnie casually washed his dirty socks. I told him it would be bad form to be late. He answered, "Not being a bookmaker, I'm not interested in form!"'

Remembering Johnnie, I realized that I had three books to return to him. They were like an index to his mind — *A Shropshire Lad*, *The Ballad of Reading Gaol*, and the stories of Ambrose Bierce.

'Yes, I must write to him,' I repeated.

The climb along the gorge brought Scotland to mind and the two men I had rested with on Ben Nevis.

'We've lost some good chaps,' I said.

Bill nodded slowly, but, looking down on the far, sinuous

road, he made no comment. Though he did not express it in words, I felt then and during the whole afternoon that to him life appeared a secondary thing, a thing so frail that death, whether it came now, or later, was something neither tragic nor terrifying.

We began climbing down the hillside, but the things of which we spoke then are no longer clear in my mind. But very clearly I recall the atmosphere of the open, English air and the warmth of Bill's nature. The wind was fresh and pure; there was no sound of aircraft; we saw no one. I remember that Bill showed me the photograph of a girl. His possession of it astonished me. In the past the world of women had been almost unknown to him. He smiled at my surprise.

'The big one should come next week.'

As we reached the road the rain increased, driving us to a sort of cleft in the gorge for shelter. It was an uncomfortable place, but dry and protected from the wind. Not until long after did I remember the other man who had once sheltered somewhere in the same gorge.

I never saw Bill again. A long time after these days I read of him in Max's diary: 'Saturday 24th April: This morning I heard the worst news the war has brought me. Bill Charlton is missing on Stettin. It is unreal. I cannot grasp or believe it. I sent a telegram to "Stiffy" just to make sure, and it was so. 460 has lost eleven crews in sixteen days.

'The news brought me a feeling of weariness, of futility, of bitterness. With one breath I felt that I must give it all up, must run away and hide before some new blow strikes me. With the next I felt a surge of anger, something that drives me to want to operate ...

'That is nine of the Twenty. It is with a strange sense of detachment that one sees the list narrow and wonders if oneself will be the next. Now and then I feel that it is all a bad dream, that suddenly I shall wake up and find myself in the canteen at Edmonton with the juke box playing "Concerto for Two" and all the boys lining up for toasted tomato sandwiches and hot chocolate.

'Bill, the gentlest, hardest working, most conscientious and most loveable of all — now a name. To some, just that — a name in the casualty lists. To those of us who knew him, a flame that will burn steadily in our memories while ever we hold to life.

'Life goes on. If we did not have something to fill our minds we would go crackers ... I went ahead with the usual preparations for the target. Five minutes before it was due to start, the operation was cancelled.

'Now I have come back to the billets and am trying to think what to say if I write to Don. Maybe I'll just read some blood and thunder yarn and keep my mind from "Stiffy's" brief telegram, "Yes, that is correct."'

Three months later we learned that Bill had been buried at Stuttgartbad, Canstatt. There were no survivors.

As we parted at Cheddar, I dismissed all apprehensions for Bill Charlton from my mind. Perhaps my optimism sprang from the knowledge that three crews at Elsham would be nearing the end of their tours and that our own total stood now at twenty. Operations were beginning to appear less a game of chance than a game of skill, and in this game both Bill and I were becoming experienced.

I left Burnham next morning to spend the remaining days of my leave at the Charlwood rectory. Although it was only my third visit to the village, I went with a feeling of possession and affection. My welcome was becoming warmer with each visit and on the evening of each arrival we were tending to sit longer over the study fire. That night I fell asleep with only the hoot of an owl to break the silence. Beyond my window the tower of St Nicholas chimed the hours as the night passed.

In the morning I heard birds waken in the garden woodpeckers, thrushes, blackbirds and, on the pond beside the drive, a solitary duck. Looking out I saw that spring was enveloping Surrey already, hiding Charlwood beneath its first leaves. This, I decided, would be the life I would choose to live, life in this small village with its family associations and its tranquil beauty. Always to see the church tower at the end of the Street; always to watch the elemental things, the seasons, the births, the deaths. To die in places such as this seemed easy. The past, with its reminders of life's brevity, was always so near that death became as natural a thing as the flow of the seasons.

Breakfast was brought to me as I sat in bed: porridge, eggs and bacon, toast and marmalade and, at my elbow, *The Times*. I had every intention of writing to Johnnie Gordon, but instead I walked each day in the sun and talked each night over the study fire.

Thus passed our last leave from the squadron. I knew that in six weeks our end would be decided.

CHAPTER NINE

Austin's Twenty-Ninth

For the first time since we had begun operating I returned light-heartedly from leave. At the Elsham gate the guard was muffled to his chin and heavily gloved.

'Good leave, Chiefie?'

'Very good,' I said. 'How have things gone here?'

'Bad, damn' bad — three crews 'ad it.'

I stopped beside him.

'Who?'

He mentioned two names I barely knew, then the third.

'Austin went on 'is twenty-ninth.'

When I did not answer he said, 'It was 'ardly fair. Five they did in seven nights. That brought Austin's crew to twenty-eight. Then they sent 'im to Berlin. It's so long since we've 'ad a crew come through, you'd think they'd let 'em do a couple o' easy targets at the end — they used to on my last squadron.'

I stood against the gate, sick at heart. 'Never curse a scrub,' he had said. 'It might have been the op you were to go missing on.'

'Are there ops tonight?'

'Yes, due in round twenty-three 'undred.'

Geoff, I found, was not yet back. Our empty room, that had reflected our gaiety when we had left, was now drab and lonely. I left it for the mess. The Station Warrant Officer, beribboned and florid, sipped his beer before a half-dead fire. I settled beside him, speaking infrequently. I began to doze. We were on the tennis court again at Nareen, resting after a singles. It was midsummer and very hot. I said to Jim, 'You know, I never imagined we'd see this spot again.'

The 'planes were overhead, their roaring tossed by the wind. I jumped up, uncertain for one insane second whether that life was real, or this. I walked to the operations room to hear the news of each arrival. Under the fluorescent lights lay a map of Europe on a long table. Other maps hung on the walls, but one wall was taken up by a large blackboard. On this were the names of the crews on the night's operations.

Instinctively I looked for Austin's name, so long familiar among the senior crews at the head of the list; but instead I saw Greig and Roper and, further down, Lay, who was Max's pilot. Opposite each pilot's name was the letter of his aircraft, the time at which he had taken off and, waiting to be filled in, the time of his return. The Waaf looking after the board was engaged to Greig's W/Op. I asked her where the crews had been.

'Hamburg,' she said. 'The first ones should soon be down.'

The 'phone rang as she was speaking. She answered it, then turned to the board and chalked after Roper's name the time 2305.

'Lay is in the circuit,' she said.

I decided to go to the crew room to meet Max Bryant. By the time I had reached it, he had come in, tired and grimy, but effervescing boyishly. He shouted to me across the room. 'Nearly up to you, Maestro - five ops in seven days!'

'How has it been?'

'Damned hot tonight, but not as bad as last night. We got mixed up with Emden and they really plastered us. A shaky do here, too.'

'Oh?'

'We lost a kite on fighter affiliation — rudders broke away during evasive action. There were nine bods aboard. Eight baled out, but the skipper went in with the kite.'

To my surprise he began to laugh.

'One type grabbed the nearest 'chute harness. It was miles too big for him. When he jumped, it slipped off his shoulders. He came down from six thousand feet hanging by one leg and dived head first into a field.'

'Killed?'

'Nope — bit of concussion. He said after that money

from his pockets hit him in the face!'

There was a stream of men trudging in now from outside, but the majority of them I knew only by sight. Flying clothing was being flung into the wooden lockers and parachutes were being taken to the drying room, while conversation flew between crew and crew. As I stood watching, I saw Roper, his parachute harness flung over his shoulder. He had poise and good looks and walked like an athlete. He had been in the RAF for a considerable time, having come, I was told, from fighters. Whether or not this was so, he always looked to me the fighter type. He was one of the few RAF men on the squadron who asserted himself with the Wing Commander and consequently was popular among the squadron's 'colonials'. I went over to him and asked what sort of a trip they had. He glanced round from his locker.

'Oh, fair enough — Chopburg seems to get progressively hotter; bags of flak and plenty of fighters. I get in and get out quickly these days. With only eight to do I put on a few extra miles an hour for the wife and kiddy.'

He glanced about the room.

'Is Jock Greig in yet?'

I followed his gaze, but saw neither Greig, nor Peter Bailey of Yeovil, nor any other member of the crew.

'They might be waiting for transport,' I said.

'Possibly — but it's not like Jock to be late.'

I remembered the Waaf at the blackboard.

'The lass on duty in the ops room is engaged to his W.Op.'

'Oh hell! Perhaps he's landed away. Are you coming over?'

Max joined us and we walked to the ops room, listening for the sound of engines.

'He'd be hard to hear in this wind,' said Max.

'Perhaps so; perhaps so.'

We entered the briefing room, our eyes contracted against the glare. In the operations room across the passage the Waaf still stood at the board. No one asked of Greig, but we saw presently that opposite his name alone nothing was written. I asked an operations officer the time limit on the crew's arrival.

'About half-past twelve,' he said. 'If they're not back then, they haven't much chance. They haven't landed away.'

I returned slowly to the crew room, still listening, but with little hope. The wind sang dolorously about the hangars and down the short, empty streets. Though the lights in the crew room had been left on, the room itself was empty. On the walls various notices fluttered in the draught from outside. I walked down the corridor, past the navigation office, past the Wing Commander's room to a door that opened on to the perimeter track. Over the unbroken expanse of grass and bitumen, the wind increased in strength, but there was no sound other than its soughing. The aerodrome lights were still on — the flarepath; the blue taxiway lights; the red obstruction lights; the sandra lights, forming a canopy over the 'drome. As I stood listening, I felt that the hangars and the woods and the very earth of Elsham itself were listening with me. Twelve-thirty came, but the wind brought no fresh sound. The searchlight beams touched a scurry of low cloud that went its way eastward as though carrying with it the secret we would never know. I waited till all hope was past. The sandra lights were doused; the flarepath was switched off. It was as though a voice had cried, 'Greig is dead!'

On the night following our return there were no operations. A crew under training took B Beer on a cross-country flight somewhere to the south. During the journey the starboard inner engine caught fire. The engine was feathered and the fire extinguished, but, owing perhaps to his inexperience, the pilot unfeathered the engine. It burst into flames again, but as there was now no extinguisher, the fire spread rapidly and burnt off the wing at its root. Six of the crew baled out, but the Yugoslavian pilot went down with the aircraft and was killed. As a minor result of this we were briefed for Essen in U Uncle.

Roper's crew were now twenty-two; Cook's and Maddern's crews, twenty each. These were the seniors. We became aware that the squadron's eyes were turned to us, filled with the hope that one of us would break the spell of disaster.

The operation to Essen was the most devastating of our tour. A year later I heard a Wing Commander of the Pathfinders declare that until this raid Krupps had never really been harmed, 'despite newspaper stories of crews who had seen their bombs fall down factory chimneys.' On this night it was a lake of flame with a small untouched island at its centre. From this island one gun put up a brave fire till it, too, was engulfed in flame.

The position on March 8th was: Roper twenty-three; Cook and Maddern twenty-one each. The target for the night of the 9th, Munich. We were operating in our new aircraft — B Baker.

'Presumably,' said the press, 'the Brown House was the target and it is only natural that the Glyptothek should suffer.'

We were never inaccurate — well, hardly ever.

March 10th, Cook and Maddern twenty-three each; Roper missing. I kept seeing him as he had been that night after Hamburg, his harness flung over his shoulder. 'I put on a few extra miles an hour for the wife and kiddy.'

In the afternoon of the next day, after we had slept, we heard that Syd Cook and Harry Wright and most of the other men of their crew had decided to continue operating with the Pathfinder Force.

I sought Harry out.

'Damn' you, what's the idea?'

He looked at me with his lugubrious eyes.

'I'm sorry t' go m'self, but we're going to have a shot at getting forty-five over in one go.' He tilted his cap on to the back of his head. 'We might be doing the wrong thing — I dunno.'

'You'll come through,' I laughed, 'I've never doubted it.'

In a few days' time the crew whose career had long run parallel with our own left Elsham for Warboys, near Huntingdon. With Harry went the conglomeration of laundry, hampers, books and boots that had been thrown under his various beds since we had left Australia together in 1941. And, from the head of his bed, went the boomerang inscribed with his operations.

I was to meet Harry and Syd only once again in our service lives. Harry was then aged twenty-three; his total operations fifty-two; his decorations, DFC, DFM. Syd was twenty-one and had the same decorations. I met Harry on this occasion along the Strand. His great coat was unbuttoned; his cap was on one eyebrow and the usual hunted, lugubrious expression was in his eyes.

'I thought you were going to do forty-five?'

'We thought we might's well keep going.'

'Till when?'

'Hell, I dunno.'

In Australia House we joined Syd. I saw that he was now a Squadron Leader. When I congratulated him, he gave his curiously boyish yet cynical smile.

'It's just a matter of survival — and we've been lucky.'

I felt then, as I had often done before, that his luck would not see him out. But of Harry I felt the opposite. On this day at Australia House I dismissed these feelings as typical of those hunches that so often came to us and were so often disproved.

Shortly after this Syd was killed on an operation to Frankfurt on the eve of his twenty-second birthday. Harry had been in hospital with sinus trouble and had not gone. He wrote to me unhappily, declaring that he would never operate again. It had been Syd's fifty-fourth trip.

Soon after Harry had left hospital he was tempted to do more. I next heard of him as a Flight Lieutenant, DFC and Bar, DFM, with seventy-seven operations on his boomerang. At that stage he left England, after operating during his embarkation leave. His total was only exceeded among the

Twenty Men by 'Tib' Barker, our course senior in Canadian training days. After a tour on Lancasters, 'Tib' did sixty-six more on Mosquitoes, bringing his total to ninety-six. He was awarded a DFC and bar.

When Cook's crew had departed from Elsham we felt ourselves isolated and watched.

'You'll be first to do it,' Max informed me.

'You think so?'

'Never doubted it.'

'What about your own luck?'

'I don't know,' he laughed.

On March 11th we returned to southern Germany, the target, Stuttgart. Unexpectedly B Baker, our new aircraft, failed us. We changed to F Freddie minutes before take-off, but the Gee was unserviceable, the astrograph was missing and there was no quadrantal correction card for the loop. We went out and returned that night mainly on our knowledge of German flak and searchlight dispositions. It brought us to number twenty-four.

A few days later I rode in brilliant sunshine to Max's room. I found him sitting outside, leaning against his wall, reading from a black-covered notebook. He looked up cheerfully. 'This must be the squadron life we used to hear praised when we were training — no ops for nearly a week.'

'Too long,' I said.

'At your stage of the game I suppose it is.'

'What are you reading?' I asked.

'My diary of our Canadian days. I must have been an innocent then. Somewhere I had the idea that people did get killed on ops, but I couldn't visualize anything happening to the Twenty. It doesn't seem to be working out that way.'

'Put it away and come for a ride.'

We coasted down a hill towards horizons magic with haze.

'This is what I feel like doing sometimes when ops are on,' I said. 'When I come to our room to pick up my things,

I imagine that I will ride hard past the barracks and out down this road. I see myself pulling up in some distant hamlet with the sound of the aircraft left behind.'

'And then, at the thought of what you had done, you would ride back up the hills and hope you would get to briefing before you were missed.'

'I suppose so.'

Where the road reached the foot of the hill there was a cattle byre with a yard enclosed by a stone wall. In the yard, which was covered deeply with straw, there were twelve or fifteen red polled bullocks feeding on mangolds which were pitched to them by a boy outside. Max asked the boy if there were more forks.

'Agin the wall there,' he answered surprisedly.

We picked them up and began pitching, growing pleasantly warm in the sun. From behind the wall came a munching and snorting and sometimes the sound of a mangold striking a bullock's head. The pitching over, we rode on, first to Melton Ross and then down steeply into Elsham village. We passed haystacks and trees bursting into leaf and pulled up at length beside the church. Above its tower rose the wolds with Elsham highest among them. The aerodrome was not only out of sight, but in the valley there was no hint of its presence. Children played in a lane that passed the church, their shouts and laughter undisturbed. Four white hens scratched industriously at the roadside grass. Max was looking up towards the invisible aerodrome.

'It's hard to believe, isn't it? — I mean the life up there. And yet, where would this England be without the other, without Roper and Greig and I suppose even us.'

In the valley the shadows came early. While the sun still touched the stacks and barns on the top of the wolds, the village fell into dusk. The children were called to their tea; the hens vanished from the road. When we returned to the aerodrome there were already signs of the fog that was preventing operations.

Next morning Max came to me unhappily.

'We've been posted to Pathfinders.'

'Oh, hell! Whose idea?'

'The Wingco's, we think. We liked this place; we're well on with our tour; you and I can keep up the old partnership — altogether it's pretty good.'

'Have you asked to stay?'

'We've tried, but the Wingco is away. By the time he's back, we'll have gone.'

We stood in unhappy contemplation of the break.

'Where are you going?'

'Warboys, near Huntingdon.'

'Lancasters?'

'Yes, 156 Squadron — the one Harry Wright and Syd Cook have gone to. George Loder is down there, too, so I won't be entirely among strangers. But still — now we'll have about thirty more to do instead of ten.'

I saw Max again that night. We walked to his room down the road I had ridden in sunshine the previous day. The night was strangely beautiful, for there was a fog no more than shoulder deep and overhead a brilliant moon. We walked down the hill, the sound of a party in the sergeants' mess faint behind us.

'Of course,' said Max pensively, 'the risk of ops aren't cumulative. There's no more reason for going on one's fifty-first than on one's first; in fact, less.'

'I remember you saying something like that once before,' I said. 'We had been briefed for Bremen in those worn-out Wimpies at Lichfield and I was too scared to imagine anything but disaster —'

'And it didn't come,' he interrupted. 'Often it doesn't. Of course, on 156 I suppose we'll have to be pretty proficient before they'll even let us operate. I believe we start by doing quite a lot of training.'

Aware of the trend of his mind, I agreed with him, minimizing the risks and plunging my head beside his in the sand. We stood talking for some time on the edge of the wood near his hut. The fog was thicker, but its level no higher than before. Its motionless surface lay white about us, descending, too, with the dip of the hillside that led to the cattle byre.

'Even so, I hate to leave. The Wingco should at least have asked us —'

His eyes, those volatile eyes I knew so well, were gazing over the strange sea of fog, as though somewhere before them lay the solution of all the problems confronting us.

'Yes, he should have asked you. When do you have to leave?'

'Nine-thirty. I suppose I'd better go — it's nearly twelve.'

'I'll see you in the morning.'

We turned away, but with a few yards between us, Max turned back.

'It was a short stay at 103, only six weeks. Still, a good six weeks.'

'Yes, very good.'

'Oh, well — goodnight.'

'Goodnight,' I said. I pushed his future from my mind.

My path led across the woods, a narrow path flanked by bare trees. Every twig and branch stood clear against the moon, but the boles of the trees were wrapped in fog. My own head and shoulders sailed towards our hut over the vaporous surface.

In the morning I saw Max go. By lunch time we had been briefed for St Nazaire, a comparatively easy step to op number twenty-five. There were now five operations left to do. During these last weeks we lived in a mood of suppressed elation. It was not wholly that the end was in sight; rather, we had crossed a shadow line and a quizzical lightness of heart was mingled with our fears as we looked into the future. We felt that we could go on for ever; that these were the finest days we would know. I saw more clearly that such men as Halford, the impassive and remote Halford, were all as the Spartan boy had been with a fox at their entrails. When first the fox attacked, few of them could suppress a gasp. But, gradually, if they lived, they learned a new bearing and a new attitude of mind. Perhaps they could not have described their attitude of mind to others, but it was evident to all those who followed them. For beginners it was a strong hand about their own. As we had regarded Fox and Kennard, so other men were now beginning to regard our crew, isolated as it was by its nearness to success.

March 26th and the target Duisburg. Owing to some trouble with B we were taking T Tommy. The pilot of T was a lean, phlegmatic Squadron Leader named Temperley, who seemed able to land at Elsham after every operation, however bad the weather. The main reason for this was that his wife lived near the station. I never remember having seen Temperley's wife; but Brian Stoker, who was his navigator, assured me that it was really she who commanded the crew. Stoker was very tall, very young and very much a public-school boy. When I told him that we were taking T Tommy, he wrinkled his brow.

'I don't like it, old boy, I really don't.

'Do you think we should see the skipper's wife?'

'It's not that. The trouble is Yohodi.' He drew me aside. 'You'd better get the gen. Yohodi is the gremlin who sees that the guns don't freeze up.'

Much to Stoker's annoyance, I smiled.

'I say now, this is pukkah gen. You'll find Yohodi on the fuselage near the rear turret. You must rub —'

'Sitting there?'

'Painted there. You can't mistake him — his name is under him. Now, this is important: you must rub his belly three times. If you don't, your guns will freeze up. We have forgotten him twice and twice our guns have frozen up.'

This was conclusive. I noted the fact with my other operational gen: Rub Yohodi's belly three times.

Stoker looked relieved.

'Have a good trip, old boy. T Tommy is guaranteed to land at Elsham in any weather.'

I had not gone far when he ran after me.

'I almost forgot. Rub the horseshoe over the navigator's

table!'

'Is that really necessary?'

'I'm warning you! If you don't want to get lost, rub the horseshoe over the navigator's table.'

I noted the matter and joined the rest of our crew in the van. Peggy, our loyal driver, took us to the aircraft. There, sure enough, was Yohodi, a fearsome being with a red and blue complexion, his baleful eyes directed astern. Geoff approached him with fitting reverence and rubbed his belly three times.

Frank regarded this performance contemptuously.

'If my goons freeze up, I'll kick yuh somewhere — an' it won't be in the belly.'

'Shut up!' I exclaimed.

When we had climbed into our places, I saw the horseshoe, a shoe that might have shod the greatest of all draught horses. As it was wired to the wall, I could see that rubbing it over the table was going to present a considerable problem. In any case, I had the impulse to throw it outside, as it was probably deflecting the compass. Concluding that the deviation card allowed for its presence, I prepared reluctantly to rub the table with it. I unwound great lengths of wire, marvelling at the trouble Stoker went to each night to placate the gremlins. At length the shoe was in my hands. I rubbed the table with it and bound it again to the wall.

The navigation that night was bewildering. The wind shifted continually; cloud was heaped without a break to 17,000ft, blanketing every acre of Europe. Nevertheless, we were one of the first to bomb and the first 'plane to return to Elsham. Stoker was waiting anxiously in the mess. As we entered he smiled broadly.

'Is T Tommy OK?'

'Quite safe — so are we, incidentally.'

'You must have done all I told you, then?'

'That damned great horseshoe! I can't understand how a man sane enough to be a navigator can have the patience to undo all that wire — '

'All that wire! You didn't — ?' He looked at me aghast. 'Don't tell me that you took the horseshoe down from the wall?'

'You said, "Rub the horseshoe over the table."'

'I meant, "Rub the horseshoe *hanging* over the table!" Rub it with your hand — the same as Yohodi's belly. My god, you've done a dreadful thing!'

Although Stoker made a joke of his crew's devotion to Yohodi and the horseshoe, I strongly suspected that, like everyone else, they would have felt uneasy had they forgotten their particular ritual — and to feel uneasy on ops was a bad thing. Geoff and Doug paid similar homage to a grimy toy rabbit, which we called 'Nunc Nunc'. Its place was above the instrument panel, where it swung like a pendulum until the operation was over. Then Geoff and Doug would solemnly kiss its rear and put it safely away until our next flight. The ground crew, too, had their superstitions. Once, after we had smuggled Joan on to B for a flight, Oscar confronted us solemnly.

'It's no good. I've seen it 'appen too often before. Good crews, too.'

'What's no good?'

'Women. At least, not in 'planes. It's askin' f' trouble. There's only one thing y' can do — pour a bottle o' whisky over the control column.'

'Cheerfully,' supplemented 'Misery'.

'Cheerfully,' corroborated Oscar.

This was stopped by Ted to whom whisky was the staff of life.

Joan had been on compassionate leave for a fortnight and there was a possibility that she might leave the WAAF. Her mother, who was an invalid, had worsened. And so, as we entered the last days of our tour, she was at her home in Liverpool, at the other end of the earth. Although each successive operation strengthened my bonds with the crew, many free evenings closed now in loneliness. To consider a walk to Barnetby and up out of its valley to 'Beacon Hill' was to be pulled up coldly.

On the 27th March we were briefed for Berlin. When take-off time came, B failed us. We changed quickly to G George, but left a good deal later than the other aircraft. Near the Dutch coast Doug located carburetter trouble in two engines.

I heard an angry intake of breath from Geoff. 'Will they hold out for the trip?'

'I think we'll lose height. If we get as far as Berlin we'll be very low.'

'Well, what do you think? Would you advise going on, or not?'

The rest of the crew were silent while the aircraft plunged into the east.

'You would never cross the North Sea, even if you got back to it from Berlin.'

'If there's one bloody thing I hate it's getting out this far and then having to turn back.'

'Well —'

'No, your opinion is good enough for me. Navigator, if I lose height we should be able to pass under the oncoming aircraft.'

We turned away from the blotched sky over Rotterdam and headed back to base. Less than an hour later we climbed out of the aircraft at Elsham, feeling like truant schoolboys. School was in and the playing grounds were empty. The Engineering Officer met us at our dispersal. After a few moments inspection with Doug he told us that we could have made no other decision. At the same time the sergeant of our ground crew found a coolant leak in a third engine.

In the morning the Wing Commander sent for Geoff and Doug. Without waiting for explanations, or seeing the Engineering Officer, he said, 'I have reported to Group that you failed to reach your objective through lack of determination.'

Shortly before this both Geoff and Doug had been recommended for commissions. Their papers were now to go no further. When the Engineering Officer took their part, the Wing Commander modified his report. We had failed to reach the target owing to 'faulty manipulation'. As far as he was concerned the commissions were still to go no further.

We were briefed again for Berlin two nights later, a night of low cloud and rain. Over Europe we were promised no better. Take-off was to be early. At 6 o'clock we walked to the crew room in steady rain, glancing upward at cloud that reflected the obstruction lights on the hangar roofs. In our hearts we clung to the belief that the operations would be scrubbed.

At 6.30 Peggy started the engine of our van. As we climbed in and began trundling away, Graham burst out with a song of ours addressed always to Peggy because Geoff rode with her in the front seat. It was a song demanded now by superstition, as it had been sung for at least twenty departures.

'Do not trust 'im,
Gentle maiden,
Though 'is voice
Be low an' sweet —'

We laughed and joined in. The rain beat against the canvas sides of the van, reminding us of the night.

We had patted the 'cookie', as was our customary habit, before getting into the aircraft, when a car drove out from control.

'Operation postponed!'

'For how long?'

'For two hours — wait in the mess.'

By the time we reached the mess, it was fully dark and raining heavily. The crews had taken off their flying clothing and were lolling in the chairs like men reprieved. We had been told to return to the crew room at 9 o'clock, but at 7.30 the tannoy demanded that we report immediately. By now the weather had become so forbidding that our reaction to this order was optimistic. It could mean nothing other than a scrub. On the way to the crew room I ran to the operations block to confirm our hopes.

'A scrub?'

An operations officer shook his head. 'Command is determined that you'll go.'

I ran through the rain to the locker room, put on my harness and collected my charts and instruments. In the crew room the rest of the men were talking cheerfully, none of them ready to leave.

'The ops people say we'll go,' I said.

'Like hell we'll go!' someone retorted. 'Just listen to that rain! The ceiling's about a hundred feet.'

As he spoke, the Wing Commander entered behind him. He glanced angrily about the room.

'Why aren't you men ready? You'll be leaving this room in five minutes.'

I sat there alone, listening to the tramp of departing feet on the concrete floor and to the constant undertone of rain. A met man carrying a bundle of forms 2303 came in. He glanced about through wet spectacles and mopped water from his face.

'Where are the crews?'

'Dressing,' I replied.

He looked anxiously at his watch, then turned to his bundle of forecast forms and passed me the one marked B. The forecast was gloomy in extreme: cloud heaped on cloud to 15,000ft; a front across the North Sea; a low icing level. The men came back, dressed to leave, their laughter silenced. The navigators collected their met cards and turned to their incomplete flight plans. The Wing Commander interrupted them sharply.

'You must leave immediately. Navigators can complete their flight plans in the aircraft.'

Outside the rain continued to fall. Overhead I could see nothing beyond the gleam of red obstruction lights on the roof of the nearest hangar. Peggy was waiting for us near the small van, her greatcoat collar turned up about her face. In a few moments we were speeding between the blue taxiway lights, singing our song as though our lives depended on it. Soon after the engines had started I felt a prod from Graham.

'Here's the 500.'

He thrust a grimy file of papers into my hand to be passed to Geoff. A moment later they came back with 'G. Maddern' pencilled in the usual place, indicating his acceptance of the aircraft. Oscar of the ground crew, who had brought them, stood waiting behind the bulkhead, his round, shining face strangely lighted by the cabin lamps. He took the papers and raised his thumb to those of us who could see him. I followed him down the dim length of the fuselage to close the door behind him. He dropped to the ground and turned facing me, bent double in the slipstream. His mouth moved, but his words I had to guess, 'Have a good trip!' I pulled in the metal ladder. Oscar had become an indistinct figure pressing through the gale of the slipstream. I slammed the door and locked it, sealing us carefully within our metal coffin.

When I had plugged in my headphones I heard the voice of the duty controller. This was unusual, as we were observing radio silence.

'All aircraft stand by! The flarepath is being changed to runway zero six.'

'Hell, there'll be some fun now!'

In a few moments an aircraft broke silence.

'Control from H Harry, permission to switch off — my engines are overheating.'

There were sharp exchanges with control, then the pilot's abrupt decision, 'H Harry — I'm switching off!'

Other aircraft began reporting the same difficulty, but the more experienced men were silent. On other aerodromes the same trouble was being reported. A wind change along the east coast had necessitated the change in direction of take-off. In many cases whole lines of 'planes standing nose to tail had to turn about in the darkness. On one squadron this resulted in such chaos that the operation was cancelled;

on another, only three got away. At Elsham we were more fortunate, only two crews failing to take off.

At 0040 Berlin filled the southern horizon.

'Not as bad as the Valley,' remarked Doug drily, 'Not as concentrated.'

'I don't need it no more damn' concentrated than that!'

'How long before we bomb, navigator?'

'Three minutes.'

'Funny; it seems quiet.'

We continued towards the target, but although we reached the edge of the searchlight belt, the city remained unmolested.

'Did you check your watch, navigator?'

'At final briefing — so did you.'

'Well, I make it forty-two and the attack was supposed to start at thirty-eight.'

'Forty-two is right. Probably the Pathfinders have boobed.'

'We'll wait out here until something happens.'

For fifteen minutes we circled Berlin. We did not know then that the attack had been put back fifteen minutes; somehow the message had never reached us. For those fifteen minutes 103 Squadron had Berlin to themselves. At fifty-four a Pathfinder marker was laid. A Lancaster dived on it and the attack began.

We heard next morning that double the weight of bombs had been dropped as on the worst raid of the London blitz. Thirty-three aircraft were missing.

The Group Captain sat rotating his swivel chair slowly, his long cigarette holder between his teeth. Possibly because of his authority over us we felt him to be older than his years. Always he was the 'old Groupie', though to us it was as much a term of affection as of age. Somehow we found it hard to believe that he had won his DSO, DFC, in the early days of this same war. Nineteen thirty-nine and nineteen forty we felt to be a decade ago.

After pocketing our pride, the members of our crew had applied for commissions. Geoff and Doug, 'lacking determination' as they did, had got no further than the Wing Commander. For me this was the second of the three necessary interviews.

'Why haven't you applied for a commission before?'

The question disconcerted me.

'I did not know it was something for which one applied,' I stammered.

'You could have had someone put you up had you wished, you know.'

He walked to the window and spoke looking away from me.

'How do you feel about operations?'

'It's hard to say, sir. Hopeful, but not over-confident.'

'Not afraid?'

'Why do you ask? Do you think——'

'Do I think you are afraid?' He was looking out the window still. 'Of course you're afraid. A man who said he was not afraid I would call a liar.'

He turned to me again.

'No, I asked because I have been wondering how you senior men have been feeling since we lost Austin, Greig and Roper.'

I tried to express our feelings, but he did not appear to hear me. He was looking out of the window again. Evidently he was thinking still of his three senior crews, for I heard him say quietly, 'I never expected it; never expected it.' Finding me still there after a few moments of silence, he said, 'Very well, I'll put you up.'

The last two days of March brought equinoctial gales. The wind howled through the wood near our barracks, scattering small branches along the road. Every few hours the tannoy uttered warnings of storms and cancellation of flights.

Only one 'plane operated. The circumstances were unusual and more than usually tragic. We had a new

Squadron Leader named O'Donoghue, a permanent RAF man who had operated in India by daylight. His crew once remarked that he disliked night operations strongly. The defences of Germany did not deter him, but he was evidently unable to accustom himself to going out in darkness, as a man suddenly stricken blind is afraid to venture outside. We who had been born blind did not understand him and were amazed when one night he asked permission to go out alone at dawn. When he made this request, operations had been cancelled owing to weather. Very early in the morning the sound of a single 'plane roused us. By the time we were up, O'Donoghue was back. The papers announced that night that a lone Lancaster had raided a town not far inside the German coast.

O'Donoghue's navigator was Flight Lieutenant 'Taffy' Davis, the man who had inspired many of us in our Lichfield training days with his ability and his carefree spirit. He had come to 103 for his second tour.

During the gale weather O'Donoghue was granted a second attempt. Again we heard him depart in the most melancholy hours of the morning, the roar of his engines torn by the wind. But by the time we were up on this occasion he had not returned. Though we waited expectantly, we heard nothing more of his aircraft. It so happened that 'Taffy' Davis had been unable to go with him. At 9 o'clock the tannoy called all crews to the briefing room. A listening post in England had heard a Lancaster calling for help. It had been hit as it crossed the enemy coast, homeward bound. Group believed that it may have ditched in the North Sea and ordered us to search an area east of the Wash. Our chances of success were obviously negligible, as met had forecast waves of 30 to 40ft high. All the morning we scanned the changing mountains and valleys of the North Sea. White-caps rose and broke, lashed by squall after squall. Eventually we flew back low across the scudding windmills of Norfolk with little hope that anyone would have anything to report. When we reached Elsham it was to hear that the German radio had claimed a single heavy bomber shot down. All members of the crew, they said, had been killed. Perhaps the listening post had heard O'Donoghue's last call; perhaps they had been mistaken.

By the time the gales had abated, April had come with its promise of better weather. On the 3rd I wrote that we were to go again to Essen, 'our seventh trip to the place and our twenty-eighth operation. The papers say now that there are "3,000 anti-aircraft guns in the Ruhr; 500 searchlights; 50,000 troops and hundreds of night fighters." We think it sounds like an underestimate. At present I am sitting at an open window in the mess, the curtains before me lifting in a spring breeze. Opposite this building is a farmhouse, once, I suppose, isolated on the summit of the Wolds. A woman there has just hung out her washing, bringing to me a feeling of nostalgia for the other life. As Max once remarked, one feels nostalgic for strange reasons in this life; in his case because through his bedroom window he could see a few hens scratching contentedly in the sunshine. Such moments make me vow that if ever again I can enjoy plain things I shall be forever grateful.

'Last night Joan returned from Liverpool, an event so unexpected and so delightful that I forgot every other aspect of our life. As ops were off I was able to meet her in Barnetby and walk with her up over Beacon Hill and back by the "lane of springy turf".

'Looking at her walking beside me, I realized afresh how large a part of my strange existence she has come to fill. Separation is now approaching swiftly. Either we will fail to survive, or we will be posted from Elsham and then I would rarely see her.

'I noticed that her usually mobile lips were compressed.

'"What are you thinking?"

'She answered immediately, "That soon you will leave Elsham."

'"After six months we may come back," I said.

'She stopped me. "You must never come back. I

shouldn't say so: I should encourage you, but I can't. To have you here would be wonderful, but sometimes it has been almost unbearable."

'Tonight I only saw her in passing and could do no more than nod when she looked at me with enquiring and apprehensive eyes.

'*Later*: The worst raid ever. We came through unscathed, but the flak was more intense than anything we have seen. One moment I remember clearly, as it showed something of Geoff's make-up. As he tried to find a way out of the target area, a fighter dived at us through flak and searchlights. In the intensity of the moment, Frank shouted a warning in his broadest Lincolnshire accent. Even as he spoke, the fighter passed below us and vanished. I heard Geoff's reply, punctuated by close shell bursts. "Frank, you must speak slowly and distinctly, or I cannot understand you." From Frank came an awed, "Yes, Geoff."

'The papers say we bombed at the rate of twelve tons a minute. Twenty-one crews were lost.'

We got to bed at 4am and twelve hours later were briefed for Kiel. Despite 'Taffy' Davis's memories of naval gunfire there early in the war, anything less than Essen seemed almost restful. By 0150 our twenty-ninth operation was over. It was now exactly five weeks since Austin had been killed on his twenty-ninth operation, which meant that we were the first four-engine crew at Elsham to come so close to the end of a tour. After the 'lack of determination' episode we felt that the Wingco would probably demand from us the full thirty operations and we would have been disappointed had he suddenly decided to screen us.

While we waited for our last briefing, Ted and I were sent to Binbrook for our final interview for commissioning. The board consisted of Group Captain Hughie Edwards, VC, DSO, DFC, and two Wing Commanders. I remember the day now for its glimpse of one of the leading men of Bomber Command. When I saw him, I felt that Hughie Edwards could almost have been awarded the VC on appearance. He looked the personification of courage.

Edwards and such other men as Gibson, Cheshire and Pickard were mountains, far above our heads. We, who had merely a tour behind us, were foothills; above us again were men of two and even three tours, but towering over us all were a few Himalayan names, men with a richer combination of skill and luck than comes to more than one in ten thousand. Below us were the broad plains, the average men of Bomber Command, for squadron life had convinced me that the average man, however great his skill, reached no more than ten operations before he was lost to sight. At Elsham the stream of average men flowed before us still. But for us, the anguish of seeing them vanish had lessened, for most of them we barely knew. In seven months we had reached old age and our contemporaries were dead. The public seldom heard of these missing thousands; rather they heard of those whose luck lasted sufficiently long for their courage to be revealed. Probably no one realized this more clearly than did the Himalayan men themselves and yet, knowing the odds, men like Edwards strained their luck to the uttermost — and seldom did they win.

April 7th, and operations were on again. On a morning of strong westerly winds and hurrying cloud we sat in the mess, moody and impatient. Frequently other men stopped to express their hopes for us, or their envy.

'Wish we were in your place! What does it feel like?'

To which we returned, superstitiously rather than sagely, 'It's as easy to go on your thirtieth as on your first.'

But we knew within us that if tomorrow we still lived, we would certainly have six months of comparatively normal life before us; possibly a year; perhaps a lifetime. Tonight would tell. Tomorrow the squadron would be elated by the promise held out by our success, or in despair because of further evidence that thirty was unattainable to Elsham men.

Geoff was more than usually irritable. He flared at me, 'Listen, go and find out what the target is.'

Leaving the crew hunched moodily over their tea, I went to the office of the operations clerks. The sergeant there was preparing escape equipment; but he spared me a friendly glance.

'So Maddern's crew has only one to do — the first thirty for seven months at least.'

I came to the point — 'The crew isn't very happy. If they knew what they were up against —'

The sergeant shook his head, 'Sorry, I just can't tell you.'

'Listen, Eric, we value our hides too highly to breathe a word—'

'I'm sorry.'

He went on with his work, while I stood undecidedly nearby. Presently he addressed an LAC standing beside him.

'Where did I put those target maps?'

These maps showed the target area in detail and on operations were used by the bomb aimer for the final run in.

The LAC answered, 'In the corner there.'

'Oh yes — beside the wireless.'

I crossed the room; glanced at the maps, then turned back to the door.

'Thanks,' I said.

The sergeant looked at me enquiringly.

I returned to the waiting crew and quietly pronounced the word they were waiting to hear: 'Duisburg!'

'Hurray!'

Why they cheered I was by no means sure, for as a target Duisburg was as bad as any we knew.

CHAPTER TEN

Final Operation

Perhaps anything we are doing for the last time we do with regret, or, if not regret, with sharp memories of all the times that have gone before. Perhaps thus we acknowledge our mortality.

In the darkened briefing room I looked about the many men, their faces indistinct in the light of the projector and the haze of smoke. Involuntarily I sought the Austins, the Foxes and the Laings of yesterday, but instead I saw strangers, strangers and a few crews who had struggled to their twenties and seemed like boys at school who were greatly junior to ourselves — Kemp, Bickers, King, Burton.

I recollected Burton's first operation. He and his crew had been driven with us to the waiting aircraft. He told us many weeks later that he had overheard our conversation.

'Burton! Good lord, how could a man survive with a name like that!'

Laughter.

'Anyway, the last three crews that have shared a bus with us have all got the chop the same night!'

'Hell, so they have — all gone for a Burton!'

Further laughter.

Burton and Harding his Canadian navigator peered at the screen, listening to the usual recitation of defences, Pathfinder plans and weather. So it would go on after tonight had passed; so it might go on for another generation in another war against another enemy.

'We have not yet got the enemy colours of the day, but should have them for final briefing.'

I stood behind Geoff and Doug as we taxied out, hearing again the hiss of brakes; the fury of motors; the mad babble of the radio. And the quiet, detached voices.

'You've got your green, Skipper.'

'Thanks, Doug. Everyone OK? Here we go!'

The intensified roaring; the thrust against our bodies; the shrinking flarepath; the vanishing buildings and woods. Though it was possible that we would come this way again, it was equally possible that never again would we leave the Elsham runways to gain height over the familiar woods and barracks to set course in the Lincolnshire sky. Though the old tension was with me still, I regarded the passing miles and the target itself with a strange detachment, as though these places no longer concerned us. Rather, my mind was in the past, even while I worked hurriedly to keep us clear of present dangers.

Over Duisburg high cloud swirled continuously, hectically lightened by flak, but blotting out all view of the target. We bombed in silence, took our photograph and turned away. On the long run to Caen, Geoff mistakenly set course ten degrees east of the heading I had given him. As we neared the French coast, still flying above cloud, he discovered his error. At the same time the Gee clarified and I fixed our position. We were on track. A ninety-miles-an-hour wind that had blown us out had eased considerably — a fact I had not discovered.

'Fifty miles to go,' I thought, 'and we'll have won.'

I visualized meeting Joan. I would go quietly to the M/T room, where she had said she would wait. She would probably be sitting alone there by the stove, while the drivers brought in the crews.

'It's cauld in this damned tooret, Maddern. What about losin' height?'

'We'll stay at fifteen thousand till we cross the coast, Frank.'

'Hell!'

Her chin would be cupped in her hands and her hair would be across her cheeks. I would open the door soundlessly and watch her a moment while she listened to the circling 'planes. Then I would say quietly, 'It's all over!'

'Maddern, lis'en, I don't know if I'm Arthur or Martha

up here. What about descendin'?'

'I've told you already, Frank, we'll hold fifteen thousand till we've crossed the coast.'

'All right, then; all right!'

She would get to her feet, not knowing whether to laugh or to cry. Then she would try to ask the usual commonplace question, 'Have a good trip?' And suddenly she would be in my arms, our ops days over.

Across the astro-dome there was a sudden brilliant light. I realized immediately that a fighter close in had opened fire. Geoff already had the nose down, flinging me among papers and instruments to the roof. I caught a glimpse of Graham pinned to the astro-dome, his eyes comically indignant.

'Have we lost him?' I waited on the gunner's replies, but Frank suddenly laughed. ''e's still 'ere — an' e's nice an' warm!'

'Holmes, you bloody fool, if you fired that tracer I'll—'

'Calm down now, Maddern. 'ere's the coast coming up.'

I switched off the Anglepoise lamp and went to the astro-dome. Behind us the mysterious land of all our adventure was slipping into darkness; the land that held the secret of the missing; the most tragic land in the world. Except for shell bursts and the watchful beams of searchlights, it was soon enveloped by night. I fancied that in the 'plane there was an inarticulate spirit of humility and gratitude.

'Set course 354 degrees magnetic for Dungeness.'

Fifteen minutes ahead of time and easily first aircraft in, we reached Elsham, singing.

'Quiet while I call control! No — you call them, "Shag".'

And so, the announcement of which Geoff was so proud he gave to his rear gunner.

''ello Hazel control; B Baker. Over!'

I imagined those waiting in the watch office, wondering if tonight would see a change in the dismal fortunes of the squadron. Out of the darkness a Waaf's voice rose in a final caress.

'Hello B Baker, this is Hazel control. QFE one zero zero fife. Pancake! Pancake!'

I raised a flask of coffee to those in my photographs.

At evening, on the border of Somerset and Devon, I came to an inn called 'The Anchor'. Alone there, I ate a meal of ham and eggs, then went upstairs to the room the landlady had prepared for me. I leaned on the sill of the open window and looked out on to the fields and hedges of the Exe valley. A quiet so deep was there that I fancied I could still hear the echo of engines and urgent words. We had been in a storm at sea, knowing nothing but noise and confusion and the death of friends. And then, at the end, we had found ourselves cast on a strange and beautiful shore. The sounds of the storm had subsided, leaving a calm that overwhelmed the senses. Our only desire was to lie as the waves had left us, absorbing the warmth of the sun.

'An English spring before us,' I said.

I remembered a moment of a few hours before, when we had shut off our engines for the last time. I remembered the congratulations, the laughter, the kisses, the cables home, the mad party with the ground crew, the wistful question asked by a youngster as he slapped our backs, 'What does it *feel* like? Just tell me that — what does it *feel* like?' It was numbing, isolating and inspiring of gratitude.

Outside my window the Exe caressed its stones. I went downstairs and out the door and crossed the bridge into Somerset. Two small boys were fishing intently on the far bank. Behind some cottages I found a lane that led uphill through sunbeams and eddies of gnats. So narrow was it that wagons had touched the hedges on either side, leaving golden stalks of hay among the leaves. I climbed slowly, for I had walked all the afternoon, following the Exe from Tiverton through Cove and Bampton to Exebridge, deviating often through inviting lanes. Now it was 9 o'clock. The lane rose steeply till it brought me to a hilltop with only the sky beyond. Standing there, I heard a faint sound that set my heart pounding and turned my eyes to a veil of cirrus in the west. There, very high, I saw a Lancaster. A surge of pride and strange sorrow swept over me. I stood listening till the sound died, then turned back to Exebridge through the lanes.

I was recalled from Somerset to the squadron. With the exception of Geoff and myself each of the crew had been posted to a different station. Geoff and I were to return to Lichfield, but, even then, Geoff was to go to the new satellite of Church Broughton. Never again were the crew to be together. Much to Geoff's astonishment, the Wing Commander had recommended him for a DFM. As Frank said, 'An' so 'e bloody well ought!' In due course he received it and later added to it an AFC.

That night I met Joan in Barnetby and told her of the posting. She clung to my arm, saying little as we walked up the hill from the village. She led me to the gate of the Saxon church and there stopped for a moment and faced me.

'You kissed me here one night, the night after Keith had gone. Somehow I remember that, because it seemed your worst time.'

We went to the seat at the west end of the church and sat there looking across the valley of Barnetby. Though the sun still touched parts of the village, most of the valley had by now fallen into shadow deepened by a layer of smoke from the cottage chimneys. Beyond the village the wolds rose towards the setting sun, ageless and gentle. A solitary windmill stood small and black against the sky. As we sat there I heard a sound from over the wolds, distant, aggressive and growing in volume.

'The aircraft are running up,' I said.

We listened till the first Lancaster rose over Elsham and began to climb. It came nearer till it banked above our heads, the sun glinting on the canopy. I imagined the bomb aimer looking directly down on to the church and two minute figures beside it. I knew the crew's emotions, the very expressions in their faces. A second and a third machine rose over Elsham, while the first gained height. Now the sonorous song of their engines filled the valley.

The first was by now flying high. I imagined Geoff's voice again, 'Oxygen on, please, Doug.'

And Doug's drawl, 'Oxygen on OK, Skipper.'

That was very long ago. I had the curious feeling that either the operational life or the life of the present was unreal; that Geoff and Doug and the other men of the crew belonged to another life known only to my inner consciousness.

Twelve aircraft in all rose over the wolds. The first had almost reached cruising height, still within hearing, but scarcely visible to our eyes. Rapidly the others joined it, till all twelve circled at 15,000ft, their roar hollowed by the amphitheatre of the sky.

'How long before we set course?'

'Five minutes to go,' I said.

'I'll turn back towards base. Ted, tell me when you see the 'drome.'

'Yes, Geoff — at the moment we are over Reade's Island.'

Presently the aircraft turned into the east.

'I'm setting course, navigator — now!'

My heart contracted.

'They're setting course,' I said.

I felt Joan's hand on my arm.

'God bring them back,' she said.

The sound faded rapidly till only to the practised ear was there a murmur of their passing. Except for a deepening of the shadows in the valley, the scene about us was unchanged. The smoke hung over the roof-tops; Gallows Wood lay newly green on the opposite side; the windmill stood dark on the rim of the world. Only then did I see that Joan had been weeping …

In the morning I heard that Bickers' crew had had a shaky do the night before. The rear gunner had been killed and for 'Bick' himself there was talk of an immediate DFC. Their 'plane had been attacked by fighters and damaged beyond belief. In the crew room 'Bick' was being congratulated. To everyone he gave the same brief answer, 'It was a crew show. The way they stuck together got us back.' Looking at Bickers, I felt that in him our past seven months were typified. For a Flight Lieutenant he was more than usually young. His face was finely formed and unsmiling; his eyes direct. And in his eyes was that enigmatical ops expression I had noticed so often before. I wondered what he had been before the war. I thought of him as a bank clerk, a university student, even a schoolboy, but each was poles removed from the Bickers before me. It was as though he had been created to wear the battered ops cap; the battle dress with its collar whistle; the white ops sweater; to be a man to whom years did not apply. But most of all, it was as though he had been created for this very hour, to stand in this drab room of many memories hearing the congratulations of his fellows.

He was the last individual I remember clearly of those on the squadron, for that day we left.[1]

For the first time since I had crewed with Geoff I was alone. The Lancaster that had brought me to Lichfield had vanished, leaving me on the perimeter track carrying my belongings. I began to walk to the sergeants' mess, alternating between loneliness and a newly discovered joy, the joy of facing an English spring without fear, the joy of knowing that I was free to turn to books, to plan for the morrow, to wander through fields. Life spread unendingly before me, more enchanting than it had ever been before. But with the eye of my other mood I saw that this life was empty of much that it had previously held. Each familiar turn of the road suggested men I had known seven months before, whose companionship I could no longer share. Near the mess I came within sight of the very hut we had left for Bremen. Beyond it was the boundary of the camp and 2 miles beyond that, the triple spires of Lichfield, rising unchanged and, in their spring setting, more than ever beautiful. That only seven months had passed seemed fantastic. Rather it was a period

---

[1] S/Ldr Ken Bickers was killed on 25.3.1944 during his second tour with 103 Squadron.

immeasurable in time. The thousands of graphic moments on the squadron had been so impressed on my mind that the period might have been seven or even twenty-seven years. Between the huts and the mess men wandered as they had done before. Nearly all of them were my own countrymen, carefree, enthusiastic and friendly. I saw them coming from our old hut and from Alan Kennedy's hut, the hut in which he had played the 'Skye Boat Song' to us on his chanter. The springtime beauty of England, the memory of Elsham, the sight of men coming to fill the places of our friends — these things combined into something bewildering and strangely moving.

I reported next day to Squadron Leader Rosevear, who had been Senior Navigation Officer in our time and was Senior Navigation Officer still. He greeted me warmly, asking after each man of our course by name. As I told him of them, he shook his head.

'It's grim, all right; it's grim.'

But his enthusiasm for operations quickly carried him away. What was the latest gen? What were the fighters like now? What did I think of Lancasters? I could see that he longed to operate again himself and thus was the ideal man for the position he held. Enthusiasm and understanding were his two finest characteristics.

'You'll be in the flying section,' he said. 'Come round and meet the boys.'

He took me through a narrow concrete corridor to a door marked in chalk, 'Kelly's Brickyard'. As he opened this door chaos confronted us. In a room perhaps 15ft by 12ft, a cricket match was in progress accompanied by intense barracking. Batting was a diminutive Flight Lieutenant who wore a DFC. He stood about 3ft from a wall bearing a large map of England. Bowling was a man as large as the batsman was small. The ball sped down the short room and was cut neatly among paper and inkwells.

'A four to Campbell,' shouted a man beside us, 'a beautiful square cut. And now Kobelke takes the ball again and goes back for his run.'

The crash of the ball hitting the stove drowned the commentary. Next I heard, 'This broadcast is coming to you from the Brisbane Cricket Ground. Your commentator is none other than the Great O'Shea.'

At this point somebody noticed 'Rosie'. A crestfallen silence descended from the pitch to the outfield. Kobelke laughed awkwardly.

'Getting a bit of practice, sir. Campbell has been chosen in the Services side for the next Test.'

'Rosie' suddenly smiled.

'I've brought you a new man,' he said. 'Try not to mislead him.'

He introduced me: Campbell, Kobelke, O'Shea, MacDonnell, Shade, 'Windy' Gale, and a few more industrious personages who had been attempting to correct navigation logs along the boundary fence. Evidently I was the prey they had been seeking. Very apologetically Campbell asked me if I would mind flying that same night. They were a bit short of men, so if I could help them out—

During this conversation I noticed that only one man in the room wore RAF uniform — a tall, fair navigator, thin and very pale. He stood with his back to the stove regarding the others with faint amusement. He was a Flight Lieutenant and wore a dilapidated DFC ribbon. Addressing me he said deliberately, 'You know, of course, that you are being trapped? While you do their flying, these clots will be down at the 'Goat' drinking their heads off. Even by Australian standards they are the poorest —'

The men of 'Kelly's Brickyard' rushed at him, but he eluded them and slipped out of the room. A second later the stove at which he had been standing blew up, showering white dust through the Brickyard. The cricketers mopped their faces and brushed their uniforms. Cockton, I gathered, was a maniac; Cockton was completely flak happy. That was twice today. Fair dinkum, 'Rosie' should do something about him.

Cockton's one ambition, I soon heard, was to get back on to ops. As he had already done 134, this was, of course, understandable. I learned later that he was trained as both a pilot and a navigator, but that he seldom wore pilot's wings in case he was made a flying instructor. He had had a bar to his DFC, but somewhere, sometime, it had fallen off and had never been replaced. A few months after this, Cockton left Lichfield to become a fighter pilot and we never heard of him again. Only the station stoves testified to his passing.

That night I flew again in a Wellington. While the navigator worked at his chart, I stood in the astro-dome checking our position by the indistinct rivers and lakes and the numerous flashing beacons. A long hose gushed hot air into the dimly lighted belly, but failed to warm me. I took several turns of it about my body, drew on a pair of gloves and settled to watch for three dreary hours. By the time the exercise was over night had almost passed. Across the fields the triple spires stood over a world yet empty of human life. We walked slowly to breakfast, the first sun shining in our faces.

'This then,' I thought, 'is my new existence.'

The members of Kelly's Brickyard were mad to a man. It was a hilarious madness and the cause of it was obvious. Careering along the operational road they had suddenly been told to change direction. The turn was altogether too much for them and they were now off the road completely, charging through every object they met. The navigators of the Brickyard were not alone in this post-operational madness. The mess, as the meeting-place of miscellaneous ex-ops men, was often a place of inspired lunacy. Newspapers caught fire in the hands of absorbed readers; furniture was piled into formidable hurdles over which a series of men would fling themselves head foremost; motor-bikes were ridden indoors. It reached its peak with the arrival from Elsham of 'Blue' Freeman. After spraying some inoffensive type's room with a fire extinguisher, he was posted to the satellite of Church Broughton. What happened there we never heard, but he was quickly posted back to the main camp. An attempt to fling himself over our table-tennis table ended disastrously near the centre and 'Blue' again disappeared to Church Broughton. This see-saw existence continued until 'Blue' eventually returned to operations. There his temperament and versatility came into their own again. Before he was twenty-two he had completed his second tour.

The extraordinary thing about the men of Kelly's Brickyard was that they got their work done. Possibly for this reason 'Rosie' usually left them alone, only stepping in when the section became completely disorganized after a heavy night in the mess, or at 'The Goat's Head'. Perhaps he realized, too, that nothing was better for pupils' morale than the joyful insanity of the instructors.

I rode one evening beside a Lichfield canal. The path was of beaten earth and so narrow that the grass beside it brushed my ankles as I rode. On the opposite bank a wood bordered the water for perhaps half a mile, a place so beautiful that I ceased riding altogether until I had reached its other end. Here and there it opened into glades, but for the greater part of its length, beech and birch and oak crowded to the water's edge. In many places rhododendrons grew wild and in great profusion — mauve, purple and white — some touching the surface of the water, as though attracted by their own reflections.

On my map the wood was called Ravenshaw. I walked to its end, then rode along the path to Tuppenhurst and Handsacre, dodging under bridges wherever a lane crossed the canal. At Handsacre I turned back, reaching the wood again at dusk. A watchful silence had settled over it, extinguishing the cries of its birds. Along its edge a family of ducks was pulling in for the night.

Looking back over the years, I see this length of canal as the quintessence of that summer of 1943. Again and again I was able to go to it in circumstances happier than I could have imagined, for Joan was granted special leave from the WAAF.

One weekend she came to stay at the Lichfield Waafery.
The day had been oppressively hot, the hottest many of us
had experienced since leaving Australia. When evening came
and I was able to leave the camp, I went to the lower gate to
wait in the lane beyond it. As I sat in the shade there I saw a
girl coming from the direction of Lichfield; not a Waaf, but
a girl who wore a sun hat and a summer dress, cool-looking
in the humid air. In the distance she appeared tall and
graceful, reminding me of my first glimpse of Joan at the
'Berkley' in Scunthorpe. As I watched she took off her hat
and ran her hand over her hair. With the motion I recognized
Joan, somehow free of uniform. I stood beside the bank.
For a moment she hesitated, then waved and came on. Her
hair, released from its Air Force restrictions, fell halfway to
her shoulders and appeared fairer than I had remembered it.
Her skin had been lightly tanned by the summer sun. As we
met I stared at her incredulously. The colour mounted to her
cheeks.

'You are being dreadfully embarrassing.'

'I hardly knew you. How did you escape from the
Waafery?'

'I brought the clothes with me and changed over there,'
she said simply.

'Over where?'

She nodded towards some trees in the fields behind us.

She took my arm with the same mingling of dependence
and possession that I remembered from our walks on the
hills above Barnetby.

In the canal a barge was moving slowly, drawn by a
horse that cropped the towpath grass. On the side of the
barge the owner's name was painted in red letters on a yellow
ground, but we saw only a child at one small window and
geraniums at another. We turned towards Ravenshaw and
Tuppenhurst. Two months had passed since I had first come
this way and now the rhododendrons had lost their blooms.
The chestnut candles, too, had gone, but rowan trees were
bright with berries and the foliage of the wood had thickened.

Along the canal we found a punt moored among the reeds. As though it had been left for our use, we stepped into it, and by manoeuvring it with a board, reached a place almost concealed by the overhanging leaves of the opposite bank. We sat for a long time without speaking, Joan leaning against my knees. I could see the back of her head and the smooth curve of her cheek and a pulse, beating quietly, where her shoulder met her neck. I leaned forward and kissed the spot gently. She clasped my hand over it.

'You are happier here, aren't you?'

'I suppose I am,' I said. 'When we met in the lane I thought the same of you.'

'It's true of me. That was winter; now it's summer.'

'Did you really think we would come through?'

'I tried to think so, but sometimes, when others were lost, I had hardly any hope left. Did you?'

'Not at the beginning,' I said, 'but the further we got, the stronger I felt, until, at the end, it began to hold a crazy sort of fascination.'

'Will you have to go back?'

'I suppose so. I can't imagine Geoff waiting longer than the usual rest period.'

'Oh, Geoff's a — a —'

'A what?'

'I don't know,' said Joan lamely.

'Padre Ratledge once called him "the personification of courage".'

'He is, too. Perhaps that's just it. You'll go back soon enough without him pushing.'

'Soon enough!' I laughed. 'You should have heard him when we came to Lichfield. After two days he said he hated instructing. He wanted the crew back. We must get back on to ops at all costs.'

'And what did you say?'

'Oh, I was the wise counsellor. I said that restlessness was no real argument for going back. Did he imagine he would relax after two tours, or three, for that matter. But then he began to say that the crew would be forced back with others. He knows he'll get me that way.'

For a time we were silent, then Joan said, 'Yes, you'll go back, I expect; back to the briefings and the wet nights in Scunthorpe and the talk about who's missing.' Then she added suddenly, 'if you go back, I'll come, too.'

'You couldn't possibly.'

'But I would.'

I turned her toward me, my hand behind her head, and kissed her. She lay against me limply, her fair hair over my knees. Almost without us being aware of it, the colours had fallen asleep. The dark haze that follows a hot day lay along the horizon. The moon had risen, every mountain on its surface standing clear in the empty air. I saw these things, but only afterwards did I remember them. Under the branches of our bank the light had so diminished that Joan, leaning against me, appeared luminously white among the shadows.

CHAPTER ELEVEN

End of a Partnership

In June my commission came through and I was given leave for kitting up. By standing invitation, I was able to spend the week at Charlwood rectory and travel to London daily.

When I arrived I found Max Bryant comfortably installed in my bedroom. I looked at him with astonishment.

He laughed, 'I knew from your last letter that you were coming here; I had the day off, so — presto!'

His luggage consisted of a toothbrush and a razor. His usual method of travel was to carry these and a quarter-inch map, then hitch hike.

'How long can you stay?'

'Only till tomorrow morning. I have to reach Warboys before lunch, in case we're briefed for anything.'

In the evening we walked slowly to Wickerspit Field and Glovers Wood.

'How many have you done?' I asked.

'Twenty-one,' he said. 'Only nine left to do before our long leave.'

The summer richness of the countryside made ops seem far off. I glanced at Max and felt incredulous that next day that other life would engulf him.

'How about George Loder?'

'He's getting near the end. Good thing, too — he has a wife and baby to think of.'

We came eventually to Beggarhouse Lane and so descended to the village.

Before seven next morning the Rector's wife came to our room with Max's breakfast. While he ate, we talked — talked so sleepily on my part that I scarcely remember a thing we said. I only remember seeing him silhouetted against the window and saying the usual thing to him as he left, 'Look after yourself.'

About a week later I received a letter from George Loder.

'After the lapse in our correspondence,' he wrote, 'I'm sorry to have to reopen it with such bloody awful news, and only the fact that you may not hear from any other source prompts me to do so.

'Max didn't return from ops on the 11th and, of course, so far we have heard no further news.

'Believe me, I know what a blow this is to you. I feel it perhaps just a little less myself, for although I wasn't associated with him as closely as you, I was tremendously fond of him — one couldn't help liking and admiring him.

'Knowing the score about ops as you and I do, I can only say there should be some hope that the crew baled out. We were both on the same target — M — and, so far as I know, no kites were seen to go down over it.

'… I don't know whether there is anything I should or could do. Although Max and I knocked round a good deal since coming here, we never discussed unpleasant possibilities. If there is anything, will you please let me know.'

Some weeks later I heard from the RAAF casualties section: '— it is deeply regretted to advise you that information has been received from the International Red Cross Committee at Geneva to the effect that the German authorities report Flying Officer Bryant as having lost his life, his body being recovered from the sea on the 17th June, 1943.'

And so the 'old partnership' was over and the answers to his many questions were known to him.

By now few of my friends remained. Of our Twenty Men, eighteen had gone to Bomber Command. Of these eighteen, ten were missing or dead. Among the remaining seven I had two close friends: George Loder and Johnnie Gordon. Both were still operating. I had last seen George nearly a year ago when nine of the Twenty Men had held a brief reunion in Doncaster. By early December he had only two operations to do to complete a Pathfinder tour of forty-five. To help the crew reach their goal, the squadron briefed them for a 'spoof' raid on a diversionary target. This well-intended gesture misfired. In a night fighter attack, all seven men of the crew were killed. Two years later the Imperturbable's DFC was handed to the daughter he never saw.

When next Geoff proposed getting back on to ops I fell in with him and flew to Elsham to enlist the aid of 'the old Groupie'. I spent the night in a room near Max's old room, on the hill above the cattle byre, and in the morning saw the Group Captain. He promised immediately to do all he could to bring us back.

In the afternoon I went to a briefing for Berlin. After, when the men had gone to the aircraft, a crew refused to go on the operation. I had left the station before their fate was known.

Within a few weeks of Geoff's attempt to return to the squadron, Training Command had refused emphatically to release him.

'I've insulted everyone worth insulting and I'm still a bloody instructor!'

That night I wrote to Johnnie Gordon. I had met him aboard the *Monterey* on the day we sailed from Sydney. The cabin opposite mine was being shared by 'Blue' Freeman and a man unknown to me. When I went in, the stranger was lying on his bunk reading. He appeared to be about thirty and was lying at full length, enveloped in his book with an air of complete indifference to the general excitement. Noticing me in the doorway, he turned his head to 'Blue'.

'Who is this strange man?'

I found myself scrutinized by a pair of weary-looking eyes, half closed as though under glaring lights. 'Blue' introduced us. This was Johnnie Gordon. Beyond his name 'Blue' probably knew nothing, except perhaps that they had the Roman Catholic faith in common. I saw that his book was *Oedipus* in the Greek. On his table were *Romeo and*

Juliet and *The Medea*. Noticing my glance towards them, he favoured me with one sentence, 'I enjoy the murders in them.'

When Johnnie deigned to appear on deck parade — he more often locked his door and read — he wore his cap in a manner that ridiculed his uniform, and he marched in a manner that ridiculed drill. At Suva he came aboard drunk; but I recollect little more of him till our course began in Canada. Then he became renowned among the Twenty as a clown, and only those who saw him listening late at night to Beethoven or Bach, or who saw his books, knew differently.

In England we were separated, he being 'billeted among the reluctant Welsh people of Llanbedrog.' He wrote: 'The people speak Welsh among themselves and many cannot speak English. In fact, the situation is in many respects like that in Quebec. There are such people as Welsh Nationals, and they're against the war (dear me, what strange people!).'

His reply to my Lichfield letter reached me quickly.

'Your letter arrived yesterday and I'm not sure that I've yet recovered from the shock. I've often felt like writing to you, but, well you know how it is — it's a hell of a struggle to write home occasionally to report the dismal fact that one is still alive.

'I've only seven to do, but that may take ages as our skipper is now a flight commander and can only do one a week. Besides, our kite is in North Africa minus two engines. It was shot up a little over Friedrichshaven, so everyone else who was shot up, too, borrowed parts of it when we reached the other side. By this time the cowling and flaps are in the form of a gunyah housing an Arab family out in the hills.

'I've got a commission coming up, I think, but am not prepared to bet on it, as I had an argument with both the Wingco and the Groupie at the interview. Still, they didn't tell me I wouldn't get one, so I suppose I can presume to hope.'

He had progressed no further with his tour when he was knocked down in the blackout by a motor-bike. By the time he had been discharged from hospital, his crew had finished their tour, leaving him still with seven to do. He wrote to me again at Lichfield:

'I don't know a soul on the squadron now, as the place has been entirely taken over by a whole horde of cheeky new crews. I am aloof and unknown, but I've got a whole bottle of Algerian wine that I had been saving to drink at interrogation on our last trip. Since our tour ended in chaos and I'm left alone and cold, I'll drink the bloody lot myself.'

At first his letter became hilarious, then, as his mask fell away, he began writing of things nearer his heart.

'Sometimes my conscience troubles me about the blind mass-murdering of the "main force". I think Bomber Command's policy is fixed too relentlessly on mere victory by annihilation. That is impossible. Britain at present seems to lack men who can look beyond the victory. I think Bomber Command's policy, though it makes the victory more certain and earlier, may make a real peace impossible.'

Eventually, by operating with inexperienced crews, Johnnie reached his required thirty and was awarded 'the routine DFC'. As we both had leave due, he asked if he and his brother could join me on a journey I had planned to North Wales.

'George has been over here eight months now and it's a devil's own job to see him for a few hours. His squadron has been alternating between Inverness and Pembroke Dock. He is a much more likeable fellow than I ever could be, they say; though he's more practical, which is a great pity. Let me know what you think about him coming — and I mean what you really think.'

As it eventuated, they went to Tal-y-Cafn alone, while I spent my leave in bed with influenza. Three weeks later Johnnie 'phoned me.

'Where are you speaking from?'

'Lichfield,' he said, 'the "Goat's Head".'

'I'll start walking! Can you walk out this way?'

'Setting course!'

When we met it was dark. I felt as we shook hands that the spirit of our Canadian days had engulfed us. For a second it seemed as though all the Twenty Men were alive and that we had wakened each other from the same hideous dream. We turned back towards Lichfield.

'We'll go down Rykneld Street,' I said. 'It seems appropriate. If you are posted here you must go to Wall and see the traces of your precious Roman civilization.'

At first he did not answer me. Then he remarked, 'I have something to tell you — you'll probably think I'm a bit mad.'

'What is it?'

'I'm going straight back on ops.'

I stopped. 'You're *what*?'

'I'm going back — on to the Dam Buster Squadron.'

'To the Dam Buster Squadron! You're crazy!'

'I think I might be.'

'Why didn't you take your rest period?'

'I don't know. I believe I just hated the idea of giving up flying to start instructing. I think that was my motive. Honestly, I don't quite know.'

We walked on down the straight road, neither of us speaking. I said at length, 'How many ops have you to do?'

'Only three.' He spoke almost apologetically. 'They're special targets. I believe they tried the Dortmund Ems Canal after the Dam raid, but they ran into ground fog. You know,' he added, with a trace of eagerness, 'they specialize in military objectives.'

The tone of his voice reminded me of the letter he had written over his bottle of Algerian wine.

'What is your opinion of the mass bombing the main force do?' I said.

'I don't like it,' he answered. 'I suppose it achieves its purpose, but it's wrong. Now it has reached fantastic proportions and we haven't anyone big enough to stop it. I suppose it will go on until all the beauty and culture are bombed out of Europe.'

Perhaps his move had been dictated by his conscience;

perhaps it was a half-conscious atonement for what he had been obliged to do before. As well as this there was the fascination of squadron life. I remembered him as I had first known him, his only apparent enthusiasm, books and music; his protective wit and foolery; his irony on all Service matters. I fancied that now he was more attached to the RAF than he had imagined possible. This and the strange twist of his conscience were his probable reasons for going to Special Duties.

'Perhaps you could change your mind?'

'I don't think so. The posting has already been made. I think if you had come to North Wales you would have persuaded me to wait.'

'Oh, hell!'

We had reached the 'Goat's Head' and there we spent the rest of the evening over nut-brown ale. Gradually my outlook mellowed, until I was confident that Johnnie's three ops were a mere nothing. By the time I had walked back to camp, I could see that it would be a piece of cake. In a few weeks he would join me at Lichfield. No trouble at all.

On the following day we went to London. By the time we had changed trains at Rugby it was dusk and, the compartments being full, we stood in the corridor, our only light a single blue globe. As though bringing forward something that had been disturbing him, Johnnie said, 'You've been a damned nuisance about this second tour. You have made me think — and when I think, I find I don't know my own motives. Why do *you* think I volunteered for special duties? Tell me honestly now. I have such a poor opinion of my own motives that I won't mind what you say.'

I said, 'It might have been because you believed mass bombing to be wrong and this move was perhaps a sort of atonement. That and the fascination of ops life.'

'Perhaps,' he said, 'I don't know. I wish now that I had come to Lichfield, or that you had come to Wales. I might have been persuaded.'

I said after a time, 'It seems doubtful in this life that we should try to influence each other, anyway.'

We stood without speaking, rocking on our feet, hearing beneath us the endless rumble of wheels.

'After what I've done, I suppose it would seem strange if I told you that I have an inordinate fear of death.'

'No,' I said, 'I think we all have — or nearly all. I keep telling myself that this last step is probably like all the other steps we have taken — hardest in the imagining. But over the target it doesn't work. I stand petrified, waiting for disintegration.'

'It's not that,' he said, 'not a fear of physical death. I don't think that matters very much. It's what comes after. The only thing that matters is whether a man is prepared to die.'

I saw, then, his church's teaching encompassing him and I knew that nothing could, or perhaps should, be said to change his attitude of mind. But it came at first as a shock to find a man so developed, so gentle, so forgiving himself, holding the view his words had revealed. I heard him say, 'Sometimes I feel that I am ready to die, but then I realize that I am not. That is what makes me afraid.'

Two weeks after our day in London, a copy of Gilbert Murray's translation of *Oedipus* reached me, and with it, a letter. On 617 Squadron Johnnie had found a change of policy. 'Apparently there's no such thing as a 'tour'. You just stay till the war's over, or till you're over, or till you've had a bellyfull.

'Now for a bombshell,' he continued. 'So I haven't a clue about women? Well, I bloody soon better have! I'm engaged!'

I continued his letter dazedly.

'Well, now laugh, damn you! But I'm used to it. At least honour me with an opinion. Silence will be taken as consent, and I couldn't stand that. I'll get in touch with you and perhaps you would like to meet the one upon whom I have cast a favourable eye.'

The wedding was set for Wednesday 26th January. If I

'happened to be in London then', would I come?

December came and we were still not on ops. Perhaps in an effort to have himself sent from the station, Geoff was involving himself in a series of 'blacks' at Church Broughton. A woman at a nearby farm declared that she would never invite him to her home again. Somehow he had taken a calf with him to an upstairs drawing-room. As the calf's behaviour had been little better than his own, they had left the house in disgrace.

'I've got to get away from Church Broughton. It would be safer on ops.'

His proposal now was that he and I should go on to Mosquitoes. Again Training Command refused his release. Christmas came and passed. Early in January Geoff sought me out eagerly, 'I've got good news!'

'You have everything teed up to get back on ops.'

He looked crestfallen. 'Well, hell — I hate instructing. Anyway, this is the real gen. I've definitely got it teed up to get back to Elsham.'

I grasped at this eagerly.

'Now you're making me sick. You only want to get back to the Elsham Waafs. Where's your patriotism?'

'Continue the story.'

'Well, Doug's ready to come back and so is "Shag". Frank is scared that if we don't get back soon he'll have to go with someone else. Old Ted is ready. "Briggy" is the only doubtful one. He's done fifty-two, so we couldn't very well ask him to do more — he's married, anyway.'

Geoff left me with the air of a man who has procured a signature to an important business deal. I was waiting to hear more of his scheme when a letter came from Johnnie Gordon. His wedding had been postponed until the 31st January. On the Christmas Eve his brother's Sunderland had been shot down over the Bay of Biscay. It had been shadowing eleven German destroyers and, in conditions of broken cloud, had evidently moved in too close. Later, the

Navy engaged the destroyers with great success, but all the crew of the Sunderland were dead.

I remembered Johnnie saying, 'At least, George is not on Bomber Command.'

Another week passed. I was expecting word from Geoff and was keyed again to ops pitch. One day an admin officer pulled me up outside the mess.

'You've been posted,' he said with a promising smile.

'Where to?'

'Australia,' he replied.

After a moment I heard myself say, 'I can't very well go. You see —'

'You'll go all right,' he said irritably. 'What's wrong with you chaps? I've told half a dozen so far and none of them want to go.'

He did not wait for an answer, but left me dazed by his words. In my mind I saw a street and a gate, but beyond them my imagination failed to reach. A tantalizing promise of reunion presented itself, but when I went to the 'phone and rang Geoff I said, 'Look, I've got to get out of it.'

'I don't think you've got a hope,' said Geoff. 'I've heard that voluntary repatriation has been a flop — now they're posting chaps without option.'

'What about our plans?'

'They fell through, anyway. Training Command refused my release again.'

I went slowly into the mess, incredulous and bewildered. Other men had been given the same posting and scarcely one of them wished to go.

It was not for some time that I saw clearly the factors that went to make up our strange rebellion. Perhaps the greatest was our attachment to England — her countryside, her capital, her pubs, her way of life and, more than all of these, her Air Force. We who had once laughed at the handle-bar moustache and the exaggerated speech had found the life of which these things were the symbols. And that life had become our life. This had happened without weakening

our attachment to our own country. It was something added
to us and, as we were living in the midst of it, we were loath
to leave it. While I packed my trunks Geoff came over from
Church Broughton. He sat moodily on my bed.

'When do you go?'

'Tomorrow. I'm going up to Aberdeen first on leave.'

He smoked gloomily, gazing at the address on the trunks.
I could not tell whether the word 'Australia' found a reponse
in him, or whether his gloom sprang from the final breaking
up of the crew.

'Are you going to call at Elsham?'

"On my way back. I suppose it will be a station of
strangers — strange air crew, anyway.'

'Kennard and Berry have had it and Pugh went back
from Lichfield and was lost on the first op of his second
tour.' Geoff flung his cigarette butt away angrily. 'But damn
it! we should have been going back.'

Next afternoon I left Lichfield by air. As we circled the
aerodrome, I looked on to the three spires of the cathedral;
to the calm Stowe Pool; to the familiar camp of yesterday.
But most I looked on our narrow canal of the past summer,
to its gleaming water, its small bridges, its bordering wood.
But the days and the place were receding. We sped into the
north, till the canal became a silver thread and the whole
scene shrank into the distance, into the past.

At Barnetby there was frost and fog. I walked to Elsham
up the familiar road, conscious of the men who had walked
that way a year before. I recalled nights with Joan,
particularly the New Year's Eve when I had walked back
late up this same road, the realization with me that no one
had completed thirty operations for a long time. Closer to
Elsham the fog grew thicker and the frost sharper. The sun,
at first a golden disc, had become a shapeless glow. The
road was icy under foot. I passed through the gates; past the
sick quarters, where Max Burcher had lain; past the huts,
our own and Keith Webber's and Hardisty's; past the sports
ground and the cabbage field. I saw strangers walking in

small groups along the road, men who wore white sweaters under their battle dress. I heard one say, 'Another scrub. Who's coming to Scunny?'

That night, sharing a room for six, I heard the squadron talk — the drunk-up in Scunthorpe; the men missing last night; the flak over Hamburg. A boy glanced at me curiously. 'You in one of the new crews?'

I said unthinkingly, 'Maddern's crew.'

'Maddern? Can't place him,' he said.

Next day there were ops. Though the fog appeared thicker, it was expected to clear by evening and the briefing continued. I went to it and sat alone at the back of the room, watching the hundred gathered heads against the screen. Again I saw the cigarettes glowing in the darkness and heard the shuffle of feet, the coughing, the low-voiced comments of annoyance, satisfaction and fear. In the morning the sun would rise; the smoke would curl from the chimneys, but where would they be, these men about me?

'The target for tonight is Magdeburg.'

Looking at the same Senior Intelligence Officer, I began to feel that this was the only life I knew, this strange mixture of comradeship, heroism and fear; this life that everyone on a squadron appeared to accept as inevitable; everyone except, perhaps, one's closest friend.

As I came out, with eyes puckered against the light, a gunner approached me with outstretched hand.

''eard you were visitin' Elsham, so I came up.' I recognized Frank Holmes. 'I'm 'ome in Kirmin'ton on leave.'

I laughed suddenly. 'You know, when I saw you, I felt we were back on ops again!'

'Well, what about it? What about comin' back?'

'I'm going home,' I said.

The smile faded from his face. After a time he said, 'Well, I suppose that's a good thing; good for you — an' y'r family'll be glad. Still, I always thought we'd get back together —'

'We planned it — right up till last week.'

'Hell!' He stared at the ground. 'How long are you stayin'
at Elsham?'

'Only ten more minutes. I have to go to Barnetby to
catch the train — I'm going to Brighton.'

'I'll walk with you t' the station,' he said resignedly.

We passed the sports ground again and the cabbage field
and the huts. Somewhere in the fog a Lancaster was being
run up for testing, the last Lancaster I heard. The moisture
on the hedges had frozen into small icicles which were falling
with a tinkling sound on to the road. The fog was thickening
so quickly that we could barely see the guardhouse as we
passed through the gate. I found myself saying then, 'Surely
not, Never again! Surely not, Never!'

But the squadron and its men had vanished into the fog,
and when we had walked a little further it was time to part.
For a moment we were dumb, Frank staring at the ground
again. He looked up suddenly and smiled.

''ave a good trip,' he said. He went away then. Within a
month he too was dead, lost with another crew.

Two days later I saw Johnnie Gordon quietly married at
Northfield. It was characteristic of him that he should leave
it until shortly before the wedding to ask me to be his best
man, as though he imagined I might not wish to bother. I
saw them later, across the table from me at their small
wedding breakfast: the bride, slim and fair; the bridegroom,
newly commissioned and wearing the ribbon of his recently
awarded DFC.

When the wedding breakfast was over I had to return to
the city. I began to say goodbye, the knowledge with me
that I would probably not see Johnnie again before I sailed.
Mary turned to us. 'You must walk down to the station
together. After all, you mightn't see each other until we arrive
in Australia.'

As we went out Johnnie said to me, 'I've written a letter
to my mother telling her all I could find out about my
brother's death. I don't suppose it would get past the censor.
Would you mind taking it?'

'Of course not,' I said.

He handed it to me.

'Don't let it get you into trouble. If you think it necessary, destroy it.'

I put it into my pocket.

'For a time the news of George goes out of my mind and I feel that he is still alive. Then I remember and it's as though someone had turned a knife in my heart.'

We walked on without speaking, coming soon to the station. Johnnie looked at his watch. 'A train is due now.'

I began to feel oppressed by the things that needed saying before we parted.

'It's been a long journey,' I said.

'Yes.' Then he said, 'I can understand now the feelings of the men from the last war as they say Binyon's "Requiem" together. It always impressed me to hear them — "At the going down of the sun and in the morning, we will remember them."'

The train had now pulled in. As he shook hands he spoke with a note of urgency in his voice that I had never heard from him before.

'If we get through this mess, we must never let the others down.'

The doors had closed and we were speeding back through the suburbs. That night I typed his letter in triplicate, putting a separate copy in a secure place in each of my two trunks and carrying the original with me.

We had been waiting some days at Brighton for word of embarkation when news came that we would not be leaving England for a week. I wired Joan, asking her if she could meet me in Tal-y-Cafn. I had stayed there in the summer and knew no place more beautiful. She replied, 'Will arrive Llandudno Saturday evening's train.' I had a foolish feeling that all that separated us would vanish.

By the time the train reached Llandudno it was dusk. Joan stepped on to the platform, a smile of suppressed excitement about her lips. As I saw her grey mobile eyes, her hair beneath a beret, her perfect figure, I felt that this could not be real. Already we had written our farewells and in reality half the Atlantic should have lain between us. We took a taxi south along the Conway river to Tal-y-Cafn, to the mountains against the stars. Joan was warm in my arms, her hand about my neck.

'Two days!' she said. 'Two whole days!'

The days were all but past. We sat with our backs against a stone fence on the top of the peak called Tal-y-Fan, the whole coast from Anglesey to the Dee lying in sunshine at our feet.

Joan looked at me over her shoulder. 'Happy?'

'Very,' I said.

'Perhaps this place is magic. Perhaps we shall be able to sit here unchanged by time.'

But too easily I could visualize the train that was to part us, creeping along the distant coast.

'When you get back to Australia, what will happen to you?'

'I expect I will go to an OTU.'

'And then?'

'Probably ops somewhere.'

'I see. It wouldn't be as bad as Europe?'

'I don't know. The living conditions would be worse and the 'planes wouldn't be as good as Lancs. But I doubt that the ops would be as bad.'

'Nothing could be as bad as last year.'

When she stopped speaking I heard the far crowing of a cock in the valley. Other minute sounds reached us with amazing clarity, yet softly and always sadly. All things must come to an end, all things. Life was a grasping of water.

Joan looked at her watch, then rose from her place beside the wall and put on her hat. I sat watching her, poised as she was against the mountains and the sky.

'Soon all this will have gone,' I thought, 'but in my memory it can remain incorruptible.'

I saw Snowdonia leaning on the sky and the far valley of the Conway with its small hedged farms. I smelt the open grassland and the sea and that other precious scent which was Joan's own. I stood up and kissed her gently.

'Less than five hours,' she said.

'Time has caught up, after all.'

'It was sweet while it lasted.'

'No regrets?'

'No regrets. Oh, of course no regrets!'

We turned downhill again with the realization that now began the parting of our ways. Down through a Roman road; past a water mill; past a ploughman; and through the village of Roe Wen.

'Goodbye, Roe Wen,' we said.

The village fell behind its hill as we walked to the hamlet of Tyn-y-Groes, our shadows before us.

'Goodbye, Tyn-y-Groes.'

As we cut across the fields to Tal-y-Cafn we came to a curiously shaped hill that presented such an outlook down the river and to the hills that momentarily we forgot our parting. On my map it was called Bryn Cwn, which is the Hill of the Dogs. We sat there on the grass and began planning a house. Its front windows would look up the river and across the hills to Carnedd Llewellyn. They would be wide windows and they must be here, where we sat. We spoke as though such things really lay before us; as though there were neither war nor parting. Then Joan said, 'But you will forget Bryn Cwn.'

I did not immediately answer her, but as we walked slowly down to the road and saw the tide swirling up the Conway, I looked at her and said, 'No, I shall never forget.'

With that she stopped and suddenly hid her face against me.

'I know you won't, I know. But — it's no use, is it?'

I wanted to say that perhaps time would lead us together, but instead I answered almost involuntarily, 'No; no.'

'If only we had met —'she began; but her voice

ended hopelessly.

She stood back from me with an air of finality and smoothed her hair.

'Let's not talk of it. I used to think that if you came through ops I would ask nothing more. It seemed too much to ask even that.'

Dinner came and passed. The train would be nearing Betws-y-Coed. We went out into the dark, across the river and on to the station. I was going as far as Llandudno, then riding back again. In the morning I would leave for Brighton. We had the compartment to ourselves, but although my memories should be of last words, it is only a memory of a conflict with time that met its end in thirty minutes.

At Llandudno Joan sat at the open window of her train. If she were to jump back to the platform, I thought, we could remain together, knowing the touch of hands. But instead we were to be torn apart, even while the scent of her remained about me. I saw the guard's green light. If I stepped aboard, time could still be cheated. But the train was moving out quietly and Joan was looking back. I walked away, back up the steps and out on to the road. I rode up hills and sped down valleys in an unknown country. Once I asked a pedestrian the way. I startled him and he cried, 'Oh, lord, holy Moses, I didn't hear you! Yeh, yeh! straight on. Oh, holy Moses.'

So I came back to the hotel and, in the morning, left.

CHAPTER TWELVE

No More Death

I arrived in Brighton late at night. Except for the usual snooker addicts, there was no one in the mess. A barman was gathering empty glasses from the tables. Tomorrow or the next day, it was whispered, we were to leave. In the mail box there was a telegram for me. I opened it unsuspectingly. The words were these: 'Need your help urgently. Johnnie has been killed.' The signature was 'Mary Gordon'.

I looked dazedly about the mess, but realized that no one there knew him. Of the Twenty Men only five were now alive and two of the five were still operating. I dragged up the stairs and went to bed. More than once in the night I tried to place a different interpretation on those unequivocal words, 'Johnnie has been killed.'

I could not escape from Brighton until the next afternoon. It was dark when Mary met me at her door, the door we had entered on their wedding day. In the blackout I could only hear her voice and smell incense on her clothes.

'I knew you would come,' she said. 'He told me you would never let him down.'

She led me into the light.

'They landed at Tangmere on their way home from operations. When they had refuelled, they took off. They hit a hill near Chichester.'

I spent next day in London, but my only clear recollection is of a fair-haired girl who sometimes called me Johnnie.

It was nearly 10 o'clock when we parted at Victoria Station. Instead of returning to Brighton, I left the train at Horley. The last bus for Charlwood had gone, but I began walking to the rectory. I was scarcely conscious of the passing miles, for in my mind was Mary's sentence, 'He told me you would never let him down.' I felt his faith in me as a strong hand about my own. This, I knew, had been the bond between the Twenty Men. It was the bond between all men in action. It reminded me of Johnnie's words as we parted, 'if we get through we must never let the others down.' He had meant, I felt, that we should not let their lives be wasted; and I did not know how this was to be done. He who might have known, was gone.

I came to the silent village. In the churchyard the trees were bare against the sky. I passed the two stones and the words that had long been hidden there:

'God shall wipe away all tears from their eyes and
There shall be no more death neither sorrow
Nor crying neither shall there be any more pain,
for
The former things are passed away.'

Epilogue

In 1958 Don Charlwood revisited the airfield at Elsham Wolds in Lincolnshire from where he flew on his tour of operations with RAF Bomber Command. This is an excerpt from an article which appeared under the heading 'By Ermine Street to Yesterday', first published in *Blackwood's Magazine* and later in *The Lancaster at War* by Mike Garbett and Brian Goulding (Ian Allan Ltd 1971).

The afternoon was wet and windy, but by five the sky had cleared and down the long, level road I saw Lincoln Cathedral, pale over its city. I remembered it then in cruciform as it appeared to us when we had set course early for Germany, or on days when we had flown low over Lincolnshire for the joy of flying.

I stopped at the cross-roads above Barnetby village. Signposts pointed east to Grimsby, south to Barnetby, north to Elsham. I felt drawn by the Elsham road, but I turned north into the village, descending to the railway that had brought us to squadron life in the autumn of 1942 and had taken us away again. The war had come and the war had gone and there was little change there. I climbed the other side of the valley to a disused Saxon church, sunken in its graveyard, crudely buttressed by men a thousand years dead. I had once known it well. From its mounded earth it had been possible to see aircraft lift off the Elsham runways, 3 or 4 miles away. But now I could see nothing, could hear only the thin whistle of a train in the valley, the train we had caught, no doubt, when departing for leave in London.

I had always vowed that if I returned to England, I would walk from Barnetby to Elsham as we had done before. Clearly I would have to break my vow. The rain was steady, my time limited, and the way was incredibly long. As I drove the 3 miles to the aerodrome, I marvelled that often I had walked this way to Barnetby and back again and then flown all night. Invariably, it seemed, the weather had been cold, or rain had blown from the North Sea. The trees, the hedges, the fields were miraculously unchanged; I saw a misshapen oak whose arms I had often watched against searchlight beams, a symbol, I had thought then, of the two lives we were living simultaneously.

I turned left to the top of the wolds and came soon to two brick pillars from which the cement was peeling. Here, in 1942, had been our gate. Close by, the guardhouse and the sick-quarters were in ruins, overgrown with nettles. I kept my eyes turned away still from the aerodrome and the main group of buildings, fearing that all sign of them would be gone. But when I looked, I saw that the main hangar, the watch-office and the water-tower were there still, squat under the rainy sky. Nearer, the dispersal points were empty, and the runways were infested with weeds.

Most of the dispersed Nissen huts had gone, but I had the illusion that in the intact buildings ahead there must yet be men, or at least a sign left for me. Near the administration block I parked the car. From 50 yards the mess still looked inhabited. I walked through the rain and went in at the open door, all at once anticipating the smell of beer and bacon and wet greatcoats, the sound of voices. But down the long room lay ploughs and harrows and bags of superphosphate. The windows were obscure with dust and cobwebs; the cheap lining of the ceiling hung in tatters. I stood very still. Somewhere hens were clucking and rain gurgled off the roof. There were no other sounds at all. Something in the room eluded me; a deafness shut me from messages on the dusty air. I walked quickly into the rain, groping for understanding of our silenced activity, the purpose of all the courage and devotion I had once seen.

A cracked and puddled road led to the operations block, the bombing-trainer, the barber's shop, the main stores and, finally, the flight office. By a piece of irony, the long building was now a piggery. Dung was raked into piles where once we had held morning parade — as if the curses of vanished crews had been taken literally by some omnipotent being. The pigs were squealing in conference. I walked slowly to the perimeter track. The wind came clean and free across the last earth touched by our wheels.

I reached the car wet and cold. Rain was still falling steadily, but I stood for a long time, casting about again for some sign of all the comradeship and courage that had ennobled this tattered hill. At the gate I felt an urge to write across the decaying columns: 'Here was the home of 103 Squadron, RAF Bomber Command, 1941-45.'

Glossary

Air Almanac almanac of astronomical tables used in converting sextant reading to latitude and longitude.

airspeed the speed of an aircraft derived from its own power, disregarding the effect on it of the prevailing wind.

astro-navigation navigation by reference to the sun, moon, planets and selected stars.

astrograph an overhead projector used at night to project star position lines onto the navigator's chart. (Used in conjunction with the sextant.)

base beam radio beam emanating from RAF aerodrome, carrying the identification signal of that aerodrome. By following its signals, as heard through headphones, the pilot was able to home to his base.

black a case of bad conduct; alternatively, a gross error leading to disgrace.

Burton 'gone for a B.': missing in action.

desynchronized d. engines were set to run at differing revolutions. Done by German raiders to upset audio-prediction by anti-aircraft batteries.

chop 'got the c.': killed. (Hamburg was often referred to as 'Chopburg'.)

computor navigational calculator.

coned trapped at the apex of a cone formed by several enemy searchlights.

cookie 5,000lb bomb.

course (now superseded by 'heading') — the direction in which an aircraft is heading (as distinct from 'track', qv.) 'Course magnetic' is the course with allowance made for magnetic variation; 'course compass' additionally allows for 'deviation' (see 'quadrantal correction card'.)

darkie code name used when calling on the special distress frequency.

deviation the deflection of an aircraft's compass needle caused by magnetic properties inherent in the aircraft itself.

DR (dead reckoning) calculation of the position of an aircraft and of its projected position derived from the compass courses and airspeeds flown. Used when outside information e.g. from radar, —astro etc — is unavailable.

DR compass (distant reading c.) A master compass, placed well aft in the aircraft, gave readings on the pilot's and the navigator's repeater units.

drift wires parallel wires on a bombsight which are so adjusted by the bomb aimer that objects on the ground are seen to pass directly along them.

flight plan calculated courses, groundspeeds and estimated times of arrival prepared by the navigator before flight on the basis of forecast winds and known airspeeds, tracks and distances.

funnels that part of an aerodrome lighting system that led an aircraft about to land to the runway in use, hence the call 'funnels' informed control that an aircraft was about to land.

gardening mine laying. (See also 'vegetables' and 'plots'.)

Gee the first radar aid to navigation used by Bomber Command. It utilized a 'master' and two 'slave' transmitters and was used in conjunction with a special chart of intersecting curves for fixing position.

gen supposedly reliable information, hence a 'gen man' — a well-informed man.

gong decoration for service or bravery.

gooseneck flares oil-burning flares of high intensity used to mark runways in conditions of poor visibility.

gremlin mischievous spirits who aimed to thwart airmen in their various tasks.

groundspeed speed of an aircraft over the ground — i.e. airspeed plus or minus the wind factor.

Happy Valley the Ruhr. (Sometimes simply 'the Valley'.)
harness parachute h. It had four leads. Two passed over
the shoulders, two between the legs. The four met at a
release buckle below the airman's rib cage.
loop a radio aid by which the W.Op. could determine the
direction from the aircraft of a radio beacon or
broadcasting station.
Mae West inflatable life jacket named after the
contemporary American film star of ample bust
development.
met meteorology and meteorological. Thus the weather
forecaster was the 'met man'; the 'met forecast' was a
subject of constant interest to aircrew.
ops operational sorties over enemy territory (c.f. the
USAF term 'missions'.)
orbit (to o.) to turn an aircraft through 360° without
change of altitude.
pancake 'You are clear to land.'
piece of cake easy.
plots those areas in which mines (see 'vegetables') were
to be sown. Alternatively, navigators made a plot of the
route to the target on their chart.
QDM international Q Code signal giving course to steer
to reach the station transmitting.
QFE international Q Code signal giving reading of air
pressure at an aerodrome, which, if set on the altimeter of
an aircraft arriving there, would result in the altimeter
reading zero when the aircraft has landed. It is expressed
in millibars — e.g. 1013.
quadrantal correction card card showing corrections to
be applied to compass headings in a particular aircraft to
allow for the magnetic properties inherent in the aircraft
itself.
sandra lights type of searchlight, usually used in threes to
form a cone over an aerodrome, thus marking its position
in poor weather for arriving aircraft.

satellite (s. aerodrome) secondary aerodrome under the command of a nearby major aerodrome.

screen an instructor whose function was to 'screen' an aircrew pupil from error. When an operational aircrew member was drafted to such instructional duties, he was said to have been 'screened' — i.e. released for 'screen' duties.

tannoy the public address system in use on RAF stations.

tour total number of operational sorties expected of aircrew by Bomber Command: one tour — 30 ops; two tours — 50 ops (with a rest period after thirty). The Pathfinder Force tour numbered 45 ops without a rest period.

track the direction of an aircraft's path over the ground. (The wind blows an aircraft from its course-or heading-onto its track, thus, in conditions of no wind, track and course are the same.)

vegetables mines. Mine laying was known as 'gardening'; the 'vegetables' were 'sown' in 'plots'.

W/Op. wireless operator. c.f. W/AG. — Wireless Operator — Air Gunner. On heavy bombers the W/AG. was seldom called upon to exercise his air gunner training and was usually referred to as 'the W/Op.'

Other Goodall paperbacks from Crécy Publishing Ltd

Enemy Coast Ahead
Guy Gibson VC, DSO and Bar, DFC and Bar
Wing Commander Guy Gibson gives one of the most brilliant descriptions of the Dambusters raid by the Lancasters of 617 Squadron which he himself led.
256 pages, paperback 'b' format
photo section 0 907579 62 0 £5.99

Pathfinder
Air Vice-Marshal Don Bennett CB, CBE, DSO
The autobiography of the leader of the Pathfinders – the élite force designed to carry out pioneering target-marking and precision-bombing of Nazi-occupied Europe.
272 pages, paperback 'b' format
photo section 0 907579 57 4 £5.99

Wing Aflame
Doug Stokes
The acclaimed biography of Victor Beamish, the legendary Irish station commander who flew an incredible 126 fighter sorties in the Battle of Britain.
224 pages, paperback 'b' format
photo section 0 907579 72 8 £5.99

Night Fighter
C.F.Rawnsley and Robert Wright
With John "Cat's-Eyes" Cunningham, "Jimmy" Rawnsley was half of one of the RAF's leading night fighter crews, destroying over twenty enemy aircraft.
256 pages, paperback 'b' format
photo section 0 907579 67 1 £5.99

Night Flyer
Lewis Brandon DSO, DFC and Bar
The exciting story of one of the most successful RAF night fighting partnerships of the war, the book also charts the development of night fighting.
208 pages, paperback 'b' format
photo section 0 907579 77 9 £5.99

Nine Lives
Al Deere OBE, DSO, DFC and Bar
The renowned autobiography of New Zealand's most famous RAF pilot who saw action from the Munich Crisis to the invasion of France in 1944.
288 pages, paperback 'b' format
photo section 0 907579 82 5 £5.99

Wing Leader
Air Vice-Marshal "Johnnie" Johnson CB, CBE, DSO and Two Bars, DFC and Bar
The thrilling story of the top-scoring Allied fighter pilot of World War Two – 'Johnnie' Johnson.
320 pages, 'b' format paperback
photo section 0 907579 87 6 £6.99

Clean Sweep
Tony Spooner DSO, DFC
The remarkable story of Air Marshal Ivor Broom who rose from the rank of Sergeant Pilot to Air Marshal receiving the DSO, three DFCs, an AFC and other decorations along the way.
278 pages, 'b' format paperback
photo section 0 907579 18 3 £5.99

Crécy Publishing Ltd,
1a Ringway Trading Estate,
Shadowmoss Road,
Manchester M22 5LH, UK
Tel: 0161 499 0024
Fax: 0161 499 0298
books@crecy.co.uk
www.crecy.co.uk